CONTENTS

3 STEPS TO ACHIEVING SUCCESS IN ANYTHING

Do you have specific hopes and dreams that you wish to achieve one day, but have no idea how to accomplish them?

If that's the case, well, you are not alone! MOST people tend to have dreams and aspirations, but only see the vision of their dream fulfilled, without being able to create a clear pathway to actually achieving it.

Many people go through life with dreams of becoming something greater than what they are now, and unfortunately many of those dreams never come true, because people don't know what steps to take to achieve success.

So without further ado, let me give you 3 actionable tips to achieving success in ANY area of your life.

1-2-3 - Success!

If you are serious about making a change and actually achieving your dreams and goals, there are things to put in place and consider, as well as actions to take.

Mostly, success depends on a couple of things - Having a clear vision, creating a concrete plan, setting a time frame & staying consistent and dedicated.

Let's have a look at each of those factors individually!

Step 1: Clear Vision of Your Goals

One of the main reasons why people are unsuccessful in achieving their goals is because they don't have a clear vision of what they want to achieve - get your pen and paper and start brainstorming!

Brainstorm

Before you start writing down your exact goals, you need to be more clear on what it is you want to achieve.

You can do this by brainstorming, researching, and spitballing some ideas of the industry you want to move into and what it will take to make your dream a reality.

This will help your brain decide on the logical pathway to take towards achieving those goals.

Write it Down

Write down everything that you want to achieve and prioritize. During this process you should also consider which ones you really feel passionate about.

Goals can be written down in the following format:

By (this date), I want to (goal that you want to achieve).

Example: By January 2022, I want to have an online ecommerce store up and running.

One at a Time

Break down your goals in different categories from most achievable to more difficult to achieve, and start working your way from the ground up.

Avoid multitasking and simply, focus on one goal at a time, though you may have multiple goals that give you inspiring visions in your mind.

Step 2: Set A Concrete Plan

Once you have a clear vision of your goal or dream, you have to start working towards analyzing what it will actually take to achieve.

Analyze your clear vision in all of its aspects and details and try to acknowledge every step along the way that will require your attention and resources.

Create a CLEAR plan of action that is as detailed as possible - Include every asset, product, expense, as well as all the steps you have to take, to get to this end goal.

Step 3: Set Up a Time frame

Deadlines, although pressing, can be just what you need to keep you on track. Setting a strict time frame in which you have to achieve certain goals will enhance your chances of success.

Wondering how you can do this? Here's how!

Scheduling
Be very specific when it comes to time framing, buy a calendar and write down certain hours you'll be devoting to certain tasks.

This is what we refer to as "micro-management" and it is crucial for achieving ANY goal whatsoever.

You MUST know when and what you will be doing, on your way to the greater goal you are chasing.

Track Progress

Your end goal (the more difficult goal to achieve) will probably be a long-term commitment, and therefore it will be easier to reach if you break it down into smaller, more achievable, goals that can be tracked on your schedule.

Track what results your actions yield, assess how that relates to the end goal and make any adjustments if need be.

Delegate Tasks

Stick to your strengths and delegate smaller tasks to someone else - Freelancers are great to hire for one-off projects like digital designing, content writing, or bookkeeping.

Doing this will help you manage your own creative energy and put it towards the things you're good at, thus helping you achieve your goal faster.

Step 4: Consistency and Motivation

No path to glory ever came without any hiccups - what makes the difference is how you deal with those drawbacks and whether you push through tough times.

Focus by Removal

It's easier for you to achieve your goals when there aren't any distractions, simply because you are able to induce a laser-like focus!

Try and get rid of anything that might distract you from focusing on the task at hand, including constant screen time, unhealthy foods, or toxic relationships.

Find Your Motivation

In order for you to be consistent in your pursuit to success, you need to have motivation.

So, ask yourself 'What is it that motivates me?' and hold on to that reason when you face difficult times on your journey.

And remember, though motivation is important, the primary driver of success is DISCIPLINE, because it allows you to take the necessary action even when you don't have the motivation to do so.

Success!
Tour success stories are different from those of others, which is exactly why you should stay focused on your own journey, rather than comparing your path to others - for some, being a good wife and mother is their success while for others owning a multi-million dollar company is.

As long as you have a clear vision of what you want to achieve and schedule the steps in a neat and achievable time frame, there is no slowing you down!

Now get out there and put in the time and effort towards your successful future.

It is all YOU.

Notes:

This page purposely left blank for your notes

3 TOXIC BEHAVIORS AND HABITS THAT ROB YOU OF ENERGY

Every person has certain behavior patterns and habits that are, in some way, toxic for the overall quality of life.

One of the crucial things (in the context of maximizing life quality), is to recognize those habits and work on them.

Without further ado, allow us to share some of the more common toxic behaviors and habits, which can be found in the majority of the population

#1 Excessive Need For External Validation

Many people do things and make themselves look in certain ways, just to be perceived better by their peers.

This is without a doubt one of the most toxic habits on the list, as it deprives you from genuine energy and relationships with people.

When we think about what other people have to say, this mainly results in our focus going more towards the outside, rather than the inside.

This in turn leads to us feeling like we always have to meet other people's expectations, instead of prioritizing our own opinions and needs.

#2 Self-Induced Guilt Tripping

Each and every one of us, at one point goes through unpleasant experiences, which lead to bad emotions.

In many instances, those emotions unfold into a flurry of guilt-tripping, where you blame yourself for one or more mistakes you made.

Much like anything else, the feeling of guilt won't be too toxic for you if it only happens every now and then, but the constant existence in the pool of guilt will, in fact ruin you.

When you focus on what you did wrong and what could've been if you did a different thing, you basically rob yourself of all your energy that can help you do more in the future.

Without a doubt, this is a toxic habit that has taken over many people's lives.

#3 Pessimistic Mindset

One of the most toxic thought patterns is that of the pessimistic mindset - something that robs many of us of opportunities and action.

Now, I'm are not trying to make you feel guilty for being negative about things... It was not your choice to think that way in the first place!

Such mindsets are developed throughout early childhood so technically, you took that from someone else.

Even more so, the brain is generally wired to expect the WORST, so that it can prepare for whatever comes its way...

Nevertheless, this function of the brain is no longer as viable in the modern-day big cities, where opportunities (and not predators) are around every corner.

Rewire your brain and look not just into the negatives, but also the possible positives and solutions of the given problem.

Conclusion

Many of us hold a variety of thought/behavior patterns and habits, which manifest into our reality only to make it worse than it was.

Without a doubt, many of those are just a chapter of the story you keep telling yourself and it seems as if that is the only truth.

Because it seems that way, you act upon it, without even recognizing it as something toxic.

If you want your overall quality of life to improve, work on recognizing those thoughts and habits which rob you of your creative power and work your way through them!

Stay woke.

5 TYPES OF PEOPLE TO SURROUND YOURSELF WITH

You wouldn't always achieve greatness on your terms — There are family and friends who encourage you and attend to your challenges.

You could even have coworkers that are as close to you as your family members are.

Life is filled with a different caliber of people that'll help you achieve personal and professional success, based on how you measure it.

And your success will mean that those closest to you will feel its impact. Let's consider five different types of individuals that will help you reach your personal and professional goals faster.

Gratitude for the things you have indicates you recognize how far you have gone in achieving your objectives.

It's a time to reflect on what you've accomplished and what the future holds — But it is also about honoring the individuals who helped you get there.

Someone who's made expressing appreciation a habit is inclined to become very successful in their field.

Meeting people like this with whom you can speak will help you to see life in a new and modest light.

Rather than focusing on the bad and what you've not done, you should focus on what you've done.

Then you figure out how to show some thanks to people who've helped you get there.

You established your own company for a purpose, and it's most probably because you're passionate about it.

When things go rough, that ardor might diminish, aligning yourself with individuals who are committed and passionate about the same thing you do is a fantastic opportunity to pick their thoughts.

Plus, you'll also see what motivates them.

This will help you discover new and interesting ways to be more committed to your professional pursuit.

You'll probably discover that the key to their endless zeal is that they tend to look at the broad picture one more time.

Unlike the average Joe, they are not entangled by whatever concerns or tedious minutiae are on their itinerary.

The only way to get over the trying times is to be enthusiastic about what you are doing.

Look for experts that are prepared to consider all alternatives before embarking on a determination.

It could result in some very inventive thought pattern, resulting in solutions you wouldn't have considered before.

The more non-judgmental people you hang around, the more you will realize how vital adaptation is.

Drive might be hard to come by — Being surrounded by individuals who exude an aura of accomplishment and who spend time working on themselves have a profound and startling influence on you.

Affiliating with driven people might inspire you to examine your work ethics and personal habits and wonder why you aren't doing more for yourself.

Ambitious people are excellent at setting realistic objectives and achieving them regularly.

There are different ways to get inspiration — podcasts, business conferences, music, movies, quotes, books; name it! The world is filled with people who have led and done remarkable things with their lives, beat the odds, and were inspired to become a better version of themselves.

If you do not currently have someone that pushes you to be who you've been dreaming of, then it's time to seek someone who will.

Watching great videos and listening to podcasts with captivating storylines that inspire you is a fantastic starting point.

Finding someone who motivates you to become better at what you do is a great place to start when it comes to becoming the ideal version of yourself.

Conclusion
The conclusion is that you'll not find greatness by doing it on your way and on your terms only. Hence, surround yourself with exceptional people that can only help you get to your destination faster than you ever imagined. Stay away from those who constantly demean or insult you! What sort of people do you hang out with? Look deep; it's time to make some changes.

ACHIEVING EMOTIONAL BALANCE

In a dynamic world like ours, life can get so stressful and no matter how positive we try to be, unexpected turns sometimes happen, leaving us overwhelmed.

Emotions are an essential part of our being, and how we deal with both negative and positive emotions plays a major role in shaping our life. This is why emotional balance is important.

It is the ability to stabilize our feeling and reaction in the face of unpleasant circumstances, rather than reacting automatically.

Being emotionally balanced does not mean you don't have unpleasant feelings; it means you can control your reaction towards them.

If you have been feeling elevated levels of anxiety and confusion about how to handle them, there are simple, actionable steps you can apply to better control your emotions.

So let's have a look at what you can actually do towards improving your emotional balance.

Steps to Achieving Emotional Balance

Being overly swayed with negative emotions will leave you anxious, stressed and cause unhealthy reactions.

Furthermore, it can also develop unhealthy coping mechanisms, which is something you don't really want.

No matter how much you struggle with this, you can achieve emotional balance by applying the following strategies.

Being self-aware helps you identify your weak spots, cultivate healthy habits, and let go of the not-so-good ones.

This helps you recognize the emotions you are feeling and the reactions they trigger which is essential for better emotional health.

Once you recognize these emotions, acknowledging the negative feelings rather than suppressing them is a way to deal with them.

This way, you start to brew a healthy relationship with your emotions and are able to catch any automatic reaction of yours.

It is helpful to verbalize how you feel at that instant, e.g. "I am angry at this situation", "I feel scared".

Naming your emotions nullifies their power and makes you react more consciously.

If you find this difficult, try journaling, this is another way to let out your feelings.

Inadequate sleep can put you in a foul mood, which means that the body requires sufficient sleep for emotional and physical wellbeing.

Though some circumstances can cause you to promote insomnia, it is crucial to find ways to increase your chances of a good night's rest.

If you have difficulty sleeping, there are some routines you can start to improve your quality of sleep.

Try to develop a sleeping pattern and stick to it, reduce caffeine intake, and avoid taking your devices with you to bed.

Also invest in the setup of your bedroom, great lighting, and comfortable beddings, as well as pre-bed meditation and breathwork.

Finding things to be thankful for will improve your outlook on life.

It could be difficult to see the good in inconvenient situations but focusing on the positive, no matter how little, improves your emotional state.

Pause at intervals throughout the day to identify things you are grateful for.

Make sure you are genuine with your feelings, and if you don't have something to be thankful for currently, think about any moment in the past you loved.

This is a good way to achieve emotional balance.

Identifying the signs of stress and devising effective management techniques help with emotional balance.

When distressing situations occur, try to spot your reaction, and learn to pause before responding.

Your breathing can serve as pointers to your stress level if you find yourself breathing irregularly or erratically, and take deep breaths to regain control.

Meditation, Yoga, Tai Chi, and/or QiGong are also perfect stress management strategies, as it is a great tool for emotional balance through self-reflection and self-discovery.

Conclusion
Remember that the difficult times are only temporary, and are a normal part of life.
The onus then lies on you to acknowledge these feelings and find the right balance to work through them.
If you are having a hard time controlling your emotions, practicing the tips in this post will help you become more emotionally balanced, so do consider those!

Notes:

This page purposely left blank for your notes

ACHIEVING THE WORK-LIFE BALANCE

The term "balance" implies that there are opposing forces in play, each trying to pull in opposite directions.

In this case, those forces are namely, well, your workplace and your personal life.

Now, if you don't know what you're seeking to accomplish, both personal and professional, it's easy to sink to the level of overworking and soon enough, you might even start to struggle with seeing beyond your work.

This is an indication that you need to consciously decide how you want to spend your life with the limited amount of time you have and strike a balance between what will make you feel productive at work and what will enrich your personal experience in life.

Why Even Achieve The Work-Life Balance?
Having a work-life balance will enable you to be more productive and healthy and also, less likely to be affected by burnout.

In addition to that, when you achieve the work-life balance, there are a number of things you'll be able to do a number of things, including but not limited to:
- Have more control over your life
- Feel a sense of accomplishment/fulfillment
- Maximize output in every area of your life
- Improve your productivity
- Tackle conflicts with ease
- Maintain healthy relationships
- Organize your life around the more meaningful things

How To Achieve a Work-Life Balance?
In case you are close to a burnout and are looking to push yourself towards a better and healthier work-life balance, there are a number of things to consider and do.

Here are our 3 best tips you can follow on your road to that balance!

Assessment Of Your Current State

First of all, you should look at the whole range of activities that currently fill your life, as some of them may slowly be burning you out, without you even realizing it.

Make a list of your current frequent activities and map out your mental state, in order to have an idea of exactly where you are, mentally.

The first step to take towards a healthy work-life balance, is to actually acknowledge that you're out of it!

Set Boundaries

If you've come to realize that you are not in an ideally balanced state and are declining towards a burnout, it is time to set some boundaries!

In the current world where many people work from their laptops, this becomes even more relevant.

If that is the case for you, try and make self-agreements, such as:
- "I will stop working at 5 P.M."
- "I will only work as much as I need to today"
- "I will take frequent breaks throughout my workday"

Nevertheless, you have to acknowledge that there will be exceptions even to those self-agreements, so be prepared for them mentally!

Let Go & Take Time

A big part of the unbalance comes from the fact that even after we're done working and have left the office (or closed the laptop), the stress from work lingers on in our heads.

For this reason it is very important to recognize those moments and thoughts and let go of them, until it's time to be mentally involved with work, yet again.

Additionally, you should take some time each day to meditate over your current state and achieve that balance we're talking about, internally.

Remember that it all starts on the inside!

Reminder & Final Thoughts

Last but not least, keep reminding yourself that you don't live to work, you work so that you can live.

You work to live your life to the fullest, whether that means spending time on your favorite interests, hobbies, family or friends.

As the former Vice Chairman and COO of Coca-Cola, Brain Dyson reminds us with the quote:

> "Imagine life as a game in which you are juggling some five balls in the air. You name them - work, family, health, friends, and spirit and you're keeping all of these in the air. You will soon understand that work is a rubber ball. If you drop it, it will bounce back. But the other four balls are made of glass. If you drip one of these, they will be irrevocably scuffed, marked, nicked, damaged, or even shattered. They will never be the same. You must understand that and strive for balance in your life."

If this quote hits home then set your priorities right and always remember what it is you are working and striving for!

AN HOUR A DAY FOR A BETTER LIFE!

Nowadays, most people see training, nutrition and other self-care activities as something time-consuming.

But what are the things you can do on the day to day basis, without using up most of your wake time?

Well, the truth is there are MANY small things you can do on the daily basis to improve your overall quality of life.

In this chapter, I'll give you great tips and activities and it is up to you to schedule them into a convenient, one-hour routine, every single day!

If you do that consistently, that'll be nearly 400 hours of work on yourself for a year.

Guess that will give results.

What Can You Do For Your Body?

You have to realize that establishing certain habits that will nourish your body is not all that hard.

Especially when you compare that to the vast amount of things you are NOT doing.

Seriously, think about it - All your bodily functions and processes are autonomous (automatic).
- You don't have to think in order to digest
- You don't have to consciously poop (it just happens to you, but you can hold it)
- You don't control any of your bodily functions for the most part

It appears that the community of cells that your body is made up of, is just a smart organism that's trying to keep you alive and healthy.

Here's what you need to do in order to support the life of your community of cells.

Be active/Include training

Optimal health occurs when all your bodily systems are working normally and with balanced chemistry.

Following that train of thought, we can say that you can't just ignore one of the biggest systems in the body - the musculo-skeletal system.

As complex as it is, the human body was MADE to move, which is why a stagnant, sedentary lifestyle may increase the risk of worsened quality of life.

And though most people think of the gym when they hear "training", lifting weights is by far not the only activity you can and should do.

Do some weight lifting, do some body weight work or Tai Chi, some hiking, climbing, swimming, running, sprinting, etc.

Enjoy the vast variety of activities your body can do and it will thank you!

Eat nourishing foods

Though the body synthesizes many of the nutrients it needs on its own, there are certain essential nutrients that the body needs, but can't produce.

This is why eating the proper foods in the right amounts, is essential when it comes to giving the body what it needs.

Protein and fats are the two essential nutrients that play major roles in many important bodily functions.

Carbohydrates on the other hand are not essential, but can be a good tool to use when trying to optimize high-intensity training performance.

Here are our best whole food picks for you to include in your nutrition plan:
- Beef
- Eggs
- Fish
- Avocado
- Mangoes
- Dairy products
- Sweet potatoes
- Honey

If you are an omnivore, animal products should be at the core of your diet, as they provide plenty of essential proteins, fats and are very satiating, making it less likely for you to overeat.

Manage stress

Even though nutrition and movement are of prime importance for your wellbeing, stress can be the make or break factor, due to its nature.

Excessive stress shuts down the body's growth, as well as the immune system and also, kicks the heart and brain out of coherence (sync).

This inner-created chaos then translates to feelings, emotions and actions in the outer world, making your overall experience bad.

Without a doubt, stress management may sound easy, but it is not the easiest thing to practice.

Take 10-20 minutes of your day to sit down in a quiet room, undisturbed and reflect back on your day.

Analyze which stress factors were persistent and put a conscious intention to react in a different way to those things.

Remember, stress management is about an inner regulation of your reactions to things.

Conclusion

For the most part, your body works automatically and all you have to do Is use it the right way and feed it with the right food, fluids, thoughts and awareness!

From then on, all the right mindsets, actions and emotions will come into place and set a life flow of greater quality.

Are you ready to make the change?

This page purposely left blank for your notes

ATTRACTING THE RIGHT PEOPLE

Your Uniqueness Is Your Strongest Quality
We all know that relationships are a massive part of our lives.

Family, friends, love interests - we deem these people so important we often identify ourselves through them.

That's not to say this is a bad thing seeing as they have a sizable influence on each of us, both as we grow up and when we're adults.

The people we surround ourselves with can make or break not just our daily mood, but how we view the world in its entirety, as well.

These are just some of the few reasons people are so important for each of us, but one question remains a mystery for many people - How do you attract the people who are right for you?

Let's find out!

Get To Know Yourself First
You can't know if something is good for you if you don't know who you are and what you want.

To make sure you understand yourself on a level where you'll have the correct opinion of other people, you need to know the answers to a few questions about yourself first.

- What qualities do you appreciate and look for both in other people and yourself?

- What are your ideologies concerning certain essential subjects and the world as a whole?

- What character traits do you want to improve and some that you won't let change?

- What do you look for in relationships, and what are you bringing to the table?

Some of these may not be as easy to answer as others, but all of them are equally important to find the right people for you and maintain the relationships you build.

Start from yourself.

Reduce The Negativity Around You
This is certainly easier said than done, but that shouldn't discourage you, really.

Whichever way we turn it, we don't have an unlimited amount of time, and negativity in any form is at the very least a waste of it.

This, however, can be a great motivator to start enjoying life more and work on making every day better for you and the people you cherish.

An easy way to start is by questioning whether a specific action or person is making you feel okay in this exact moment and in general - by evaluating an exact situation, you have a clearer perspective on what the thing in question brings you.

From that point on, all you have to do is stay true to your feelings - this might be difficult but is worth it in the end.

Be honest about what you're thinking and feeling, and make sure the person opposite you understands you correctly.

By removing some of the negative emotions in your life, you have more time to dedicate to your ambitions, plans, and current experiences.

Embrace Your Quirks
This is where the magic happens.

Everyone's unique, and everyone has their own amazing individual thoughts, emotions, and traits, which is precisely why life is so colorful in the first place!

By staying true to what you love and embracing what you want to become, you are pushing to make your dreams a reality and attracting like-minded people in the process.

Think of this - you have undoubtedly found it impressive when people are genuine to themselves.

This is exactly because they're unapologetic about who they are and what they believe in and build their very own paths in life.

Sure they might be weird from time to time, but they're honest, and because of that, you can always trust them and their actions, which is valid for their opinion and feelings for the people they surround themselves with.

Accepting and acting the way you actually want to is a complicated process, but it's what turns you into the person you aspire to be and that, by definition, surrounds you with the right type of people.

Start Looking!
Once you have all this down, this final step is actually surprisingly easy.

You can start interacting with people that have similar interests to you and make new relationships from there.

Hobbies are great for many reasons, and this is one of them - going dancing, enjoying a sport, or wine-tasting are all social activities and most likely filled with people just like you.

And the best part is once you're honest about what you want, you waste no time in anything short of just right.

Sure, relationships can sometimes be difficult, and building new ones may sound a bit intimidating at first, but it only gets better once you start.

Key Message

Finding the social circle that's right for you will undoubtedly make your life much more happy and easy while also helping you turn into who you aim to be.

By being true to yourself, you let everyone around you know who you are and what you're looking for.

Attracting the type of people you want happens only when you're honest, and that honesty is exactly the reason behind the magnetism itself.

With all of this being said, it's time you go out into the world and indulge in your uniqueness and liveliness - the right people for you will be there to cheer you on!

This page purposely left blank for your notes

BECOMING MORE SELF-AWARE

Living in a world where we are constantly comparing ourselves to others, can have the sad result of us losing ourselves while trying to be more like everyone we see on social media.

To be authentically yourself, you have to be fully aware of who you truly are - your weaknesses, your strengths, your beliefs, your goals, your personality, your motivations, and your morals (values).

This is what you are made of and you have to realize that all of those aspects are capable of changes and improvement.

In this guide, I'll give you tips on how you can ultimately increase your self-awareness for the greater purpose of becoming the best version of yourself.

Attracting Awareness

It's easier said than done, I know! But it all starts with a suggestion to your brain, which can then get it through its filter and allow it to have an impact on how you feel, think and experience.

Let's have a look at the 4 things you can do to become more self aware!

Get To Know You
Have you ever sat down with yourself and asked the question: "Who am I?"

And more importantly… Would you be able to answer that question if it was posed?

The first step in building a healthy awareness of yourself is to understand who you truly are when you look at yourself objectively.

You can start off by writing down your own perceptions of yourself if you were to look at yourself objectively and from an outside perspective.

During this process, you shouldn't compare yourself to others, but rather look at yourself as an individual without comparisons while looking at your accomplishments, interests, beliefs, and personality.

Granted, though, you will never be able to map out your entirety on a piece of paper, but you can get to know the most frequently occurring patterns you have, that make the most of your life.

Journaling

One of the best ways to keep track of your daily emotions, reactions, and feelings is to keep a journal in which you write down those things.

It's amazing how putting pen to paper can really put things into perspective;

Writing down your feelings, thoughts, failures and successes of the day will give you a fresh view on how you deal with things.

Journaling is a means of self-reflection to not only see your strengths, but also your weaknesses as it gives you the objective perspective to change bad reactions in the future.

Recording your daily way of acting and reacting will also help you clear your mind and open up space for positive energy.

Mindful Habits
During our daily lives we can become quite robotic, as if we are on autopilot just cruising through our schedules and before we know it, weeks and months have flown by.

To savour every moment of the day, we have to be more mindful of what we do, this means being aware of good and bad habits while enforcing better habits more.

Trying to keep up with a fast-paced world can keep us from enjoying small pleasures like breathing in fresh air or simply going for a stroll around the neighborhood.

Which tasks during your day gives you a sense of serenity, calmness, and happiness?

Is it washing the dishes, meditating, cooking, or exercising?

Ensure that you do these kinds of activities more!

Ask Feedback

Even though it might be a bit scary, it's important to know what our friends, family, and even colleagues think about us and our behavior.

Ask those closest to you to give an honest and open, but critical and objective, description of who they see you as, to give you a better idea of what people truly think of you.

Honest feedback from people around us, will give us a better idea of who we are and how our behavior affects our everyday lives.

Obviously it's important that you remain open-minded and non-offensive during an honest feedback session from a friend, listening with an open heart might help you recognize something within yourself you never knew was there.

In The End

To be more self aware, switch off your devices and go inward to discover the true you.

Once you make contact with the authentic person inside, you'll in fact exit the main sequence of emotional and behavioral patterns, opening room for more new & exciting experiences.

Are you ready?

Notes:

This page purposely left blank for your notes

BURNOUT - PART 1: WHAT IT IS AND HOW IT HAPPENS

If you feel completely drained-out, helpless, tired, and lost all the time, you might be paving your way towards burnout.

Burnout is the state of being emotionally, physically, mentally, and spiritually exhausted due to excessively long periods of stress and trauma, or, well a lot of mental and/or physical work!

The term 'burnout' was made popular by Herbert Freudenberger, in 1974 in his book, Burnout: The High Cost of High Achievement.

He explained the term as, "the extinction of motivation or incentive, especially where one's devotion to a cause or relationship fails to produce the desired results."

Certain people believe that they tend to perform well under pressure, but imagine being constantly under pressure, in a constant struggle of proving one's self, we sometimes become exhausted, empty, and are unable to cope with it.

People mostly confuse burnout with stress, but there is a difference between the two. Stress is characterized by one's over-engagement in work whereas burnout is characterized by disengagement from work.

Stress can lead to urgency and a state of hyperactivity whereas burnout can cause helplessness and hopelessness.

Simply, burnout is a condition much worse than anxiety or stress, and that is the exact reason why you have to understand it.

What Is It and How Does It Happen?
As I suggested, the burnout is a state of having a void in life, where one doesn't know where to go, what to do, and how to overcome this feeling of emptiness, loneliness, and hollowness.
Burnout is usually observed among employees who work either full-time or do multiple part-time jobs.
There has been a 24% increase in the search for symptoms of burnout from the previous year and the number seems to be increasing.
Now let's look at some of the factors that may contribute to the manifestation of mental and physical burnouts.

Too Much Pressure

Working with a tough boss, assigned tasks to be unattainable, late-sittings now and then, or software that you don't know how to use, all of these situations can be stressful, and too much of that stress can lead you to the road of burnout.

Going to work daily from 9-5 in a stressful environment means exposing yourself to constant pressure which highly increases the chance of burning yourself out.

Make sure to stay mindful during those situations and CHOOSE how to respond, instead of relying on your automatic reactions, which can often stress you out!

Deadlines Over Deadlines

Cutthroat deadlines can be fun and motivating for some people as they find thrill in doing such a task.

For those people, being challenged with a deadline gives a sigh of relief once the task is completed.

Now imagine, you are barely at the finish line of your first task, and you are assigned another one?

If your supervisor/boss is only piling up deadlines over deadlines for you, it can eventually lead to a burnout, even if you love working under pressure.

Where is my Appraisal?

Remember when your mother used to reward you with your favorite food for completing your homework on time, or when you scored 10/10 on a test and received a star?

Well, we have been taught to expect a reward for our hard work whether it be materialistic, monetary, or appreciation.

However, MOST companies that employ plenty of workers, believe that payment is a sufficient stimulus.

Nevertheless, the thought and notion of living paycheck to paycheck, working a 9-5 job, is often stressful and can thus, lead to symptoms of a classical burnout.

If that's the case for you, talk with your colleagues and the higher authority figures in the company to set up better reward systems, based on working performance!

When such systems are put into place, you and your colleagues will find the burnouts to happen less often and may in fact be motivated and happy to work.

No-way Out!

People who are not happy or satisfied with their workplace tend to look for other jobs, but it's not easy to find jobs in the market and they find themselves stuck with their current employer.

In the fear of losing the job, they can't even discuss the issues with their employer and feel left out.

The feeling of no way out makes people depressed and less focused, thus increasing the probability of a burnout and even, a breakdown!

Final Thoughts

Our society is built in a way that demands workers to focus on a task for at least half of their wake time, with little to no rest.

Unfortunately, most positions you can take on, do not consider attention span & rest times between working sessions.

This, in combination with a variety of other factors, can make you exceed your working capacity, thus leading to a state of burnout.

Nevertheless, there are ways to deal with this which I will present in next chapter.

BURNOUT - PART 2: HOW TO DEAL WITH IT

Burnout doesn't only have emotional or mental symptoms but it may also carry physical harm to one's body.

Fatigue, frequent headaches, loss of appetite, lowered immunity, are just some of the unpleasant side effects you can experience during a burnout.

In this chapter I'll give you insights on how to recognize and deal with burnout, for your own, greater good!

Signs Of A Burnout

A burnout is usually the result of a gradual build-up of stress, which manifests significantly more at one point, which we can refer to as "the crash".

Oftentimes, the burnout may be lurking without you even realizing it, which is why it is important to recognize it early on.

Here are the 3 most common signs of a burnout:

Chronic Exhaustion
Don't think that you are being lazy rather identify the fact it's an outcome of burnout.
When you are burned out, exhaustion becomes a part of you just like second nature.
Think about it - Have you ever woken up from your comfy bed just to find yourself as exhausted as someone after a full workday in the fields?
If that's the case and if it happens regularly, rest assured - The full-on burnout is probably incoming...

Asociality

It is not a cold/flu/fever, that it will hit all at once. The symptoms will reveal one after another, you will start alienating yourself from others whether be it your family, friends, or coworkers. Cynicism will hit you, disengaging you from worldly joys and delights. Burning out is not a phase that will just pass, rather it will flush you away in its darkness and loneliness.

Inefficacy

When you are burned out it's hard to concentrate on work and a numbness overcomes your entire body making you lose control over your habits.

Are you feeling demotivated, discouraged, demoralized and well, just numb overall?

If that's the new anthem of your life and you feel like you're lacking the productivity and achievements you once were capable of, then it is highly likely that you are en route to a burnout!

Finding a Fix

Burnout can be accompanied by a wide range of mental and physical health symptoms, as we already mentioned.

Burnout, if left untreated, can make it difficult for a person to function well in their everyday life, so let us have a look at what you can actually do to get your body and mind back to where they were, prior to the burnout.

Seek Help

In many individuals, a classical burnout can lead to some really dark thoughts, which at the moment may seem like the right thing, because, well everything is meaningless!

However, the burnout is just a filter, through which everything appears meaningless, so this is not really all there is to the story.

To yet again find the meaning of existence, communicate your thoughts and feelings with the people around you.

We are social beings and during the darkest moments, a conversation with the right person can be a saver!

Mindfulness
Though it may not be easy to do during a burnout, try to consciously and neutrally pay attention to your inner self.
Realize that the burnout is just a state and with each breath, you are getting further and further away from it.

Be mindful even of your worst states, choose not to respond emotionally and you'll see them pass by seamlessly,

Prioritize Yourself

Put yourself before anyone else whether it be family or work. Self-care is the most important ingredient in baking a blissful life.

Prioritizing yourself is the best thing that one can do for themselves. It doesn't let other factors overpower you and creates much-needed balance in life.

Furthermore, this will help you almost certainly prevent a burnout in the future, so do pay attention to this aspect!

Focus on Meaning

If your roles and responsibilities prevent you from taking immediate time off, Halvorson recommends "focusing on why the work matters to you."

Connecting your current project to a larger personal goal (i.e finishing this project will financially help you realize an idea of yours).

However, keep in mind that this may only provide temporary relief and if that's the case, just...

Take A Break!

Think about it - How often do you happen to have a day or two, where you're literally doing NOTHING...?

In the past, human life was simple because we were bound to survival - We woke up, hunted, picked fruits and by the time we came back to camp, it was already getting dark.

However, nowadays, we have WAY more tasks of different types and that is precisely why burnout exists in the first place.

Take some days off from anything and everything and focus on the things that make you feel calm and relaxed.

This way, your body and brain will be able to rejuvenate and you'll be back at full working capacity in no time!

Concluding Thoughts
Though a burnout may be exhausting, think of it this way - It is just an opportunity to reevaluate your priorities, passions and current employment agenda, as well as... Take the much-needed break!
If you're experiencing some or all of the symptoms I mentioned in this article, just take a break and shift your focus back to your own well-being.
The secret to everything else is there - In your own, personal health and well-being.
Keep those on point.

Notes:

CONNECTING WITH DIFFERENT TYPES OF ART

What Should You Try Next And Why It's Important To Keep Exploring
Art has been a part of our lives for millennia. The first artwork ever made was of outlines of hands in 290 000 BCE in Indonesia (at least from what we know and have found thus far!)

That shows how innate it is for us to use our imagination and create something.

Different types of art later started developing alongside our intelligence and technology.

These included music, theater, paintings, books, all the way to movies and games in recent decades.

But how can you connect with art, yourself and what impact can this have on your life?

Let's find out!

The Different Types Of Art

Art is a word that evokes many different ideas, images and emotions. It can be defined as the expression of human creative skill in visual form.

Art may take the form of a painting, drawing, sculpture or other media such as a film, for example.

There are many different types of art to explore and enjoy- from abstract to figurative work, from modern to traditional, from highbrow to lowbrow.

The following paragraphs will introduce you to the different types of art that represent various artistic mediums and genres.

And so are you ready to find the type of art that most resonates with YOUR soul?

Let's go!

Visual Art

This first type of art refers to many different visual forms of art, ranging from paintings to sculptures, but not only.

You can find some unbelievable ideas being brought to life through this medium.

Go to big and small exhibitions, attend gallery openings, and search for small coffee shops that have a defined look because of the art hanging on the walls.

It's a vast area of exploration that offers some amazing stuff, both for your eyes and the soul!

Also, try to discover your local artists and support their work. It makes you a part of a community filled to the brim with exciting people!

Finally, if you want, try creating something yourself - it's one of the easiest ways to rest and get in touch with yourself.

Because after all, art is not just something to enjoy with your senses, but a medium to self-expression, too.

Music

Oh, where would the world be without music, eh?

We all have a specific music taste, and getting to hear your favorite artists live is an experience like no other.

With that in mind, try to go to world festivals, be a part of the thousands of people that attended the concert of their lifetime, but also, don't forget to cherish your local scene, too!

Many of the artists you love wouldn't be who they are if they didn't have the support from their local fans.

You can find some great musicians that are more underground and know that by supporting them, you helped them rise up.

If you really have a passion for music, try playing an instrument as well - even if you don't become a musician yourself, playing something for the first time is still a pleasant experience.

Theater
This is one of the most ancient arts, and for a good reason. Many actors in movies started in theater, and they're still a part of some plays because they love it so much.
Plays both in your language and by other authors, as well as classics have their merit.

It's also enjoyable to go to the plays of university students because they have a new approach to most characters and an immense passion for what they're doing.

You'll encounter some stories that cannot be read or seen in a different medium, which adds uniqueness to the experience itself.

You can even do some acting exercises if you want, because most of them are simple but very fun.

Books

Reading is a timeless hobby and one that has a lot of benefits. You can start small by reading some short stories and see where you end up from there.

If you can, it's also exciting to read in different languages, because it brings a new appreciation of the language or you can read translations of authors from other countries.

Here it's also essential to support your local scene, so get some books of local authors, seeing as they will probably be highly relatable.

If you want, you can keep a journal of what you've read or maybe even a storybook of your very own ideas.

Movies

We all watch movies, and it's never a bad idea to keep this hobby.

You can try international movie festivals to see some more experimental titles or watch films made in your own country.

Blockbuster titles are also sometimes excellent and are always a good point for comparison.

If you're a real movie buff, you can try thinking of a story and a script on your own or maybe some reviews and essays on your favorite shows and films.

Games

Gaming is taking up the world by storm, and for a good reason - it manages to mix pretty much all types of art.

You can try playing some triple-A titles and see how much technology has improved, or you can try some indie games and see an entirely different approach to gaming, which is usually filled with an extraordinary amount of passion.

If that's not your cup of tea, you can swing for some tabletop games and play with your friends and family.

This medium is so big and fascinating that it's pretty much impossible not to like something.

If you're feeling creative you can think of new games or different ways to use some tried and tested mechanics.

The Benefits Of Exploration

By getting in contact with different types of art, you constantly find other points of view and ways of thinking, reacting, and feeling.

Art has been a part of our world in all its forms because sometimes, to create is simply a need.

Exploring different perceptions keeps you connected with people from all walks of life.

Trying to make art yourself develops your creativity which is a big part of our intelligence and broadens your physical and mental abilities.

A cultured person's overall quality of life is often much higher than that of people who have no interest in art.

This is because creating and exploring stimulates our brain, broadens our perspective, and makes us feel, thus instigating positive changes in pretty much every corner of our lives.

Getting in touch with art also deepens existing interests, which helps us become more knowledgeable of topics we care about.

Final Thoughts

Art, in general keeps life curious and inspiring.

Whether you're exploring the most cutting-edge and innovative artists or sticking to classics, you will undoubtedly find something you love.

By trying to create art yourself, you are letting your creativity flow and in a way allowing yourself to be a kid again, which is never a bad feeling.

With all the business of our lives, it's essential to have something that helps you relax and keep you interested and motivated to explore the world.

So why not try something new, why not see that movie, go to this gallery or listen to that musician?

Why not even try to create something yourself?

So go ahead then, get in touch with art!

DO AFFIRMATIONS WORK?

How To Integrate Them In Your Life

Affirmation or self-talk is the internal dialogue with the subconscious mind of an individual, and well, the truth is that affirmations can be both a positive and a negative self-talk.

We tend to engage in self-talk in our routine by thinking or speaking about ourselves, our lives, and our current state of mind without being aware of it.

Remember that one time someone asked you to play a game and you responded "Nah, I'm too bad at this…"

Well guess what, that is an affirmation! By saying this out-loud, or even thinking about it, you just affirm to the brain that you actually suck at this and thus, your brain, actions and thoughts bend to that belief and make it a reality.

Oppositely, if you respond with "Sure, I'm pretty certain I can learn this game in no time!", you make a positive affirmation that follows the same sequence, making the brain believe it can learn quickly and again, bending to that belief to make it a reality.

So, the short answer to the question is - Yes! Affirmations do work. However, more often than not, people use them to affirm negative beliefs, rather than positive ones.

If you're looking for ways to integrate affirmations positively in your life, do keep reading.

How Positive Affirmations Affect You

Since positive affirmations are about success, positivity, and productivity, they inspire and motivate you to achieve your goals.

With positive self-talk, you are able to create a positive mental attitude by literally tricking your brain into creating new belief systems, or upgrading the old ones.

In addition to that, doing so can help you A LOT in certain situations, such as:

- It helps you stay motivated when you feel demotivated
- It inspires you when you are looking for inspiration
- You are able to develop good, positive habits
- It improves your mental health

The bottom line is that positive affirmations and positive self-talk allow you to change things for the better.

You are cheerful about life and don't feel miserable anymore, because you've managed to break into your subconscious and rewire it.

How Negative Affirmations Affect You
Contrary to positive affirmations, negative affirmations are destructive, as that negative self-talk makes you feel bad and miserable.
It does not allow you to change your thoughts/viewpoints and bring about good change.
Furthermore, the negative affirmations focus on problems and failures, rather than your ability to overcome them.
With having negative self-talk you only make the problems bigger because:
- It causes low self-esteem
- You feel little or no hope
- It reinforces the feeling of the victim
- You feel stressed

When you tell yourself things like "I am a failure" you allow yourself to feel even more miserable.

Making a Shift From Negative To Positive Affirmations

Since negative affirmations will not create any results, you must shift from negative to positive affirmations in order to live a happy, positive, and meaningful life.

As Donna Karan says, "Delete the negative; accentuate the positive!" To do this, firstly, you will need to promise yourself to accept and acknowledge the negative thoughts, rather than attach to them and make them linger on for longer.

Once you acknowledge those thoughts, try to not take them so seriously and don't let them unfold as an entire story in your head. Don't dwell on your negative thoughts.

Secondly, learn to reverse the negative affirmations. A very simple strategy to this is by replacing every negative phrase with the positive one.

For instance, when you feel like you are worthless, tell yourself that you are worthy, or, instead of saying "This is impossible to do" try and say "There is probably at least one way to do this".

Thirdly and most importantly, write down the positive affirmations for every negative one.

By doing this, you will see a shift that will make your negative thoughts disappear and you will be able to focus more on positivity.

I refer to this process as acting "As If" also. Whatever you are working to become, by acting "As If", you are instructing your unconscious mind to begin the path that leads to that outcome.

Doing Daily Affirmations

Positive affirmations are a powerful way to develop positive thoughts every day, because repeating certain phrases makes them more and more believable to your brain. The best part? Such positive affirmations could be used for self-love, work, stress-management, self-esteem, success, and more. You can find various affirmations online, but remember that developing your own, personal affirmations is the best way to actually FEEL them and thus, make them more believable for your brain. An important thing to remember and consider while developing your affirmations is you should always focus on well-meaning positivity and facts.

In addition to that, your daily affirmation should be written and spoken in the present tense because your brain communicates in the present.

Conclusion

There are a number of limiting beliefs that we hold, which lead to us affirming negative things about ourselves, out-loud or an internal self-talk.

Affirmations can make or break you, so learning how to master that self-talk is essential for your own greater good and success.

Try and analyze yourself and get rid of everything negative that you keep believing about yourself and replace it with something more likely to bring about a positive outcome.

So what are you waiting for? Start doing your daily affirmations and rewire your belief system!

This page purposely left blank for your notes

EMOTIONAL INTELLIGENCE - WHAT IS IT & HOW TO DEVELOP IT?

In the 21st century, our senses get bombarded with loads of different information, which may often cause us to react in certain, more emotional ways.

Oftentimes, this emotional response may leave us feeling lost and hopeless about a certain thing and that state can sometimes linger on for weeks and months on end.

But what is emotional intelligence and can you actually train your brain to respond less acutely to stressful situations?

In this chapter, you're going to learn more about emotional intelligence, what it is and how to take control over your otherwise automatic responses.

Let's get to it now, shall we?

By Definition...

Emotional intelligence, by definition, is one's ability to recognize, be aware and in control of their own emotional reactions and those of others.

The concept of emotional intelligence was first created back in 1995, when Daniel Goleman published a book called "Emotional intelligence".

In his book, Daniel talks about how an emotionally intelligent person is able to differentiate between his emotions and is able to use them to navigate his/hers thoughts and actions.

Though this is easier said than done, there are certain guidelines to follow if you want to take control over your emotions and reactions.

The 5 Abilities To Help You Take Control

In order to take control over your emotions and reactions and keep them regulated (instead of having them control you), there are 5 main abilities to focus on and develop.

#1 Empathy

At its very core, empathy is one's ability to put themselves in other people's shoes and understand their thought patterns, emotions, reactions, feelings and behaviors.

In doing so, you will realize that there is no ultimate truth- Everyone is bound to their own belief system and their own encoded emotional responses and thought patterns.

#2 Self-Awareness

This second ability can manifest on many different levels, but when it comes to emotional intelligence, it is in fact crucial.

Being able to recognize your own emotions, feelings, thoughts, behaviors and reactions is of prime importance when you are becoming more emotionally intelligent.

And though recognizing them is important, it is just half the battle- The other half is to actually make conscious choices and break those patterns.

#3 Discipline

In the modern-day world, it is believed that there is a "once and for all" solution to all your emotional problems/depression.

Well, the truth is that there is no such thing as permanent happiness, because as humans, we constantly surf the entire emotional spectrum, as long as we are alive!

Staying consistent and disciplined with the physical and emotional well-being practices is important when you are building your emotional intelligence.

#4 Self-Regulation

At its very core, self-regulation is an important ability to develop, which is at the very core of emotional intelligence.

This is one's ability to control their emotions and actions leading after the emotions.

And even if you lose it and fall for the automatic reactions encoded into you, well-developed self regulation would mean that you will recover much quicker, after an emotional reaction.

#5 Social intelligence

As emotional humans, we must realize that our emotional states affect others, especially when they are in our environment.

Social emotional intelligence is one's ability to control their emotions and reactions in a social environment.

Emotional Intelligence = Happiness?

As I already mentioned, there is this global idea that there are certain actions you can take, which will result in eternal, life-long happiness, with the absence of bad emotions.

However, this is simply not true!

Even more so, as social beings, we are all different and we all have a set of emotional responses and reactions.

The differences between people are a premise for problems and conflicts, but if emotional intelligence is present on at least one side, there would be a certain level of understanding, which can alleviate any personal/social conflict.

On top of that, emotional intelligence allows us to be more aware of what we feel under certain circumstances.

This therefore gives us a greater level of adaptability, which in turn helps us make the right choices in the more important aspects of life.

Take Home Message...
For the most part, humans have a specific set of encoded, emotional responses and reactions, which, for the most part are automatic.

You didn't really choose to be that way; those things were literally given to you when you were a child.

They were given to you by your parents, siblings, other relatives, teachers, friends, etc.
Emotional intelligence is about recognizing those automatic responses and asking yourself "Who gave me that and do I really need it to affect me that way?".

After setting that conscious realization, your next step is to take conscious action and take control over your emotions, instead of letting them control you.

Stay woke.

FINANCIAL DISCIPLINE - MONEY SPENDING HABITS

As the saying goes, money isn't everything, however, the absence of money can bring a lot of trouble.

This is the exact reason why developing good financial discipline is essential for your long-term prosperity.

Unless you're a financial guru of some sort, odds are that you may find certain aspects of money management more difficult.

In this chapter, I'm going to pin-point the most important considerations, which can help you develop good financial discipline.

What Is Money, Anyway?

Before you get to work and manage your money (and eventually make it work for you), you have to understand what money actually is.

Think about it, we all want to have millions, but which people actually have those millions?

People who are worth millions, plain and simple!

That is to say that money is nothing but a unified way to express the market value which an individual gives/receives to and from other people.

Check out our 6 best tips below, that will help you re-think your finances and habits!

#1 Set The Excuses Aside

Many of us have poor financial discipline, because we refuse to accept it is true.

You have to realize that just like anything else, developing financial discipline takes time and consistent effort.

This implies that all excuses must be set aside and actions should be taken, according to the goal.

Ultimately, changing your spending habits and lifestyle may be crucial to achieving balance in your finances and work.

#2 Create A Plan

Now that you've started changing your money spending habits, it is time to create a plan of action.

Analyze yourself and track down the non-essential things (like food) that take up most of your money.

If you've been spending recklessly on something you can live without, set a limit on it and come up with a reasonable monthly budget to fit everything in, starting from the most vital, to least important things.

#3 Think Twice!

In a world where social media knows you and your interests better than you know them yourself, it is quite easy to slip and go on a money-spending spree.

But do we really NEED most of the things we spend a lot of money on? Well, in most cases… Not really.

In order to minimize non-essential purchases, try asking yourself these 3 questions, before checking out:
- Do I really need this and how am I going to use it?
- Is this important for me or am I just slipping?
- Did I need this before I saw it?

If you do this, you will undoubtedly have a greater chance of estimating whether or not this product you want is worth the money.

Don't Forget, Though...

Developing good financial discipline doesn't really mean depriving yourself of all the small treats and things you like.

It is more about integrating those things into a healthy, monthly budget that also allows you to set money aside and have everything essential for your wellbeing.

Granted, if you take all the right steps towards that goal, you will set yourself up well in the long term and will be able to better manage your personal resources, which will in turn allow you to achieve and have certain things.

So, what is YOUR financial discipline like?

FINDING PEACE IN ADVENTURE

The Mindset Of A Traveler

There are many different ways one can choose to live their lives in terms of ideologies, aspirations, and goals.

These things tend to vary from place to place and from decade to decade, and they all have their reasons as well as good and bad sides.

Throughout our history, we can see that some people find their comfort in traveling.

Although most of the people that adopt this mindset don't take it to the extreme, some very impressive records have been set in terms of traveling.

The longest walk without stopping for instance took 2 425 days and was done by George Meegan between 1977 and 1983.

Another impressive feat is that of Bertrand Piccard and Briton Brian Jones, who were the first people to travel around the world by a hot-air balloon in just 15 days.

Here I give some more interesting facts about traveling as a way of life so if the above sounded exciting, keep reading!

I also explain how people like them think and why this is a wonderful mindset, albeit a little weird at first sight.

The Basics
- So, Why Do People Travel?

Travelling is connected with many different aspects of life.

People travel a lot because of work or in order to rest, one because of the different conditions foreign countries offer, the other in order to take a break from their everyday life and return home refreshed.

Different reasons can be for fun (going to specific destinations, events etc.), to visit friends that live far away, or to understand themselves better by exploring what the world has to offer.

People with the traveler mindset usually fall in the last category.

They see adventure as a mix between all the other reasons and therefore use it as a source of inspiration and a resolution for their problems.
- How Often Does It Happen?

More than 1.4 billion people are international tourists each year.

And this does not account for the people that move to live in different countries.

Today around 1 in every 30 people lives in a different place from where they were born, which shows how easy moving has become thanks to modern technology and the ability to work from anywhere.

Another interesting fact is that northern Europeans travel the most, with Finland taking the first position in international travel with 7.5 trips a year.
- What Are The Most Visited Places?

France is the most visited country by tourists in the world today.

The most popular tourist attractions are different each year, but the Eiffel Tower, Times Square, the Wall of China, the Colosseum, and the Taj Mahal are pretty much always in the top 10.

The situation is very different, however, concerning where most people move to live.

The most popular places here include Canada, Germany, Switzerland, Spain, Japan, and Qatar, mainly because of their high quality of life and good conditions both for people born there and for foreigners.

The Mindset
- What Is The Traveler's Mindset?

This is the way of thinking that predisposes curiosity, open-mindedness, and appreciation for the moment.

It's important to mention that this mindset needs a fair dose of bravery and can put some aspects of life to the test.

However, if you're the type of creative-thinker these people usually are, you will have no trouble figuring out flexible ways to deal with similar issues.

Having a sense of adventure leads you to new places and experiences, teaching you a lot about the world and yourself, and the people with this mindset put these values at the top of the list.

The traveler's mindset is based on exploration and living in the present, opposing the more common idea of always looking in the future.
- What Are The Main Reasons Behind It?

Adventurers feel a deep connection between themselves and the world and want to build their way of life based on it.

Challenging themselves in order to learn but at the same time being appreciative of everything they have and are surrounded by, are the main reasons most people adopt this mindset.

A different but also crucial aspect of it is being more understanding and feeling more connected to yourself and others as well as enjoying different points of view, habits, and ideas.

People with this mindset find it relaxing to travel and nurture their creativity and resilience, having different places be a source of inspiration both for ways of rest and hard work.

- How To Build it?

Most people with this mindset believe that the most important part of it is learning to be in the moment.

Once you have that down, taking the actions you want is much easier, and it always leads to more curious situations and places.

Learning to be okay with the ever-changing surroundings is also very important, and it teaches you compassion and resolution.

While that isn't simple if you start by appreciating the differences between each one you'll be better in no time.

Another aspect is understanding and treating yourself as well as you can - you are the master of your own journey, and it can only be as good as you make it.

Self-acceptance is one of the core reasons for this mindset to be so positive both in the sense of being good for you and making your outlook on life a better one.

With these ingredients, becoming a true adventurer is just a matter of time.

Traveling as a way of living is not for everyone.

It takes time and effort, and most of the time, it changes your life completely.

However, if you find yourself imagining living this way it's never too late or too difficult to start.

Having a traveler's mindset will inevitably broaden your horizons and teach you things both about the world and yourself you otherwise will not be able to experience.

Although it can be hard to imagine at first, adopting this way of thinking and living is proven to be one of the best and most positive decisions a person can make.

With all this being said, we hope to see you in different countries, trying different things, and exploring new horizons very soon!

Explore the world to truly understand it.

This page purposely left blank for your notes

FINDING THE RIGHT CAREER PATH

Have you ever stopped to wonder whether you're on the right career path?

Yes, I know you have and you're not the only one - All of us have been there at one point after our teenage years.

A 2020 Deloitte survey found that 31% of millennials and about 50% of those from Generation Z are planning to leave their jobs within two years.

This statistic shows how rocky the younger generation's psyche is towards snatching a stable and fulfilling job.

So then what is the alternative - we stick with the mundane job that doesn't make us happy, but still pays the bills, or we leave everything in the search of something better?

Let's find out.

Why is this happening to me?

If you think you're the only one that struggles with getting a grip on your professional life, you are highly mistaken.

The social factor in this case plays the biggest role. A lot of young people tend to rush into sudden decisions regarding their career choices.

This happens mainly due to expectations from the social and family circles. You have to find a paying job and you have to like it, there is no other way you can succeed.

Alternatively, there is always the chance that you just want to make easy money with less work, which, believe me, doesn't work like that.

So, let's look at some possible tips for changing all of this.

Let's go back to high school

Remember when in high school the guidance chancellor gave you a career personality test.

You didn't pay much attention to it then, right? But It actually could have been pretty useful.

Tests that calculate the ideal job for you can establish the working ground for your potential profession to be.

There are some pretty spot-on tests and quizzes online that can get you focused on a certain qualification that matches your personality and good traits.

While we're on the subject of personality traits, let's talk about...

Making a list, and checking it twice!
It really does help to write down the thing you want out of your dream job. It doesn't even have to ideally be your dream job, but the one you feel you will be good at.

The list may include things you are good at, things you are bad at, things you want to do as a hobby, and things you want to work.

It could even include traits that you have that are suitable for different companies. That way you will arrange your strong sides when you need to point them out to the person that will interview you.

Do not underestimate the power of making a list, because we usually tend to undermine the process of carefully sorting out all these personality traits.

Always be in touch with the times

It's important to know what is out there, as well as what job pays how much.

It sounds a little capitalistic as an approach, but you always have to remember that if you're good at something, you should avoid doing it for free!

Meet new people and don't be afraid to ask for advice.

The connections that you make with a diverse crowd will form a steady know-how approach to the job you want.

Never stop trying

It is thought and sometimes it gets even harder, but you should never fall under the pressure of caving in.

Never stop trying to reach your goals and always ask yourself why you are doing what you're doing.

You need to be very aware of the goals you want to achieve and what you're willing to give to reach them.

Final Thoughts

Finding the right career path isn't really easy - It takes a lot of trial and error, going through different positions, meeting different people and being in different communities.

At the end of the day, you should answer 2 questions for yourself:
- What is it that I'm really good at and know a lot about?
- What is it that I'd really enjoy doing for a big part of my life?

These are the two core questions that can take you a step closer to finding your career path.

How did YOU find your career path?

FULFILLING YOUR TRUE POTENTIAL

Living up to your true potential provides a distinct sense of fulfillment, and according to Aristotle in his book The Nicomachean Ethics, we all have the potential for greatness.

Realizing that potential, he believes, is the key to living a truly happy and fulfilling life, even in your older years.

Nevertheless, fulfilling your true potential and being a high-performer is a matter of developing certain skills and mental traits.

So without further ado, let's have a look at what those traits and skills actually are, shall we?!

Self Awareness

If you want to know what your true potential hides and how to get there, you must feel at ease with who and what you are.

Don't pretend to be someone you're not and don't try to change yourself solely because others tell you to.

Instead, understand who you are and what you want to be... And if you don't know, you should find out by doing things and analyzing yourself and how you feel doing them... This is the essence of self-awareness!

Read, write, think, and speak. That is self-awareness: simply being aware of your thoughts and feelings.

When you are self-aware, you automatically learn more about yourself.

It all starts with awareness.

No awareness - No knowledge!

Perseverance

Perseverance is inferred from failing and rising again. You cannot become resilient if you do not commit mistakes.

Sometimes you work and you get nothing in return. For years, you work but do not see any outcomes.

You get no acknowledgment, no money, and no rewards. But eventually, you start seeing the results you have long been waiting for.

You get better at your job and get more confidence. You even start earning more.

If this sounds familiar, consider this - if you didn't persevere, you would not get any of those things.

Writing

We've all felt a need to vent and express ourselves in an attempt to get our point across.

Writing, on the other hand, can assist you in actually achieving this. When you write things down, you become more conscious of your choice of words.

This implies that your writing will be more insightful, concise, and elegant than your speech.

Improved writing leads to improved thinking. Better thinking leads to improved communication.

Better communication translates to improved career outcomes.

So write, write, write! Whether that means writing your goals and plans down, or simply doing creative writing.

Mindfulness

Mindfulness is more about being a mindful person than it is about meditation, yoga, or Buddhism.

A mindful person is in command of their emotions and thoughts. He/she is as solid as a rock.

Someone on whom others can rely. However, achieving that inner peace takes a lot of practice.

You might think that you will never be able to fully master this skill. You can, however, improve your control over your thoughts by practicing.

The essence of the mindfulness practice lies in being able to recognize recurring patterns and taking conscious decisions at the moment of their occurrence, that is contrary to that automatic reaction.

Productivity

It is important to understand that the more present you are, the more desire you have for improving your life.

And you can improve your life by working on the things you like. Thinking about achieving your goals will not do anything real for you.

Evolve into a person who is productive every day.

Don't continue to waste it by watching TV, hanging out with the wrong people, or engaging in any other mindless, mundane activities.

Make the most of your time.

Leadership
Leadership is all about motivating people and helping them reach their full potential.

This can be done by teaching others to have autonomy and focusing on themselves.

When you fix your own problems and become a strong person you can rely on, you help others more.

When you are able to do this, you inspire others to do the same.

It is only the selfish and narcissistic people who want to make people dependent on them…

Leaders believe otherwise!

Final Thoughts

If you've started doing something, do it to the best of your ability or don't do it at all.

That is the quickest way to realize your full potential and it's also the most difficult.

That, however, should come as no surprise to you. If you don't succeed the first time, learn from your mistakes and remember Henry Ford's words:

"Failure is simply the opportunity to begin again, this time more intelligently." – Henry Ford

HABITS - WHAT THEY ARE AND WHY THEY MATTER

Origin, Explanation And Why They're So Important

Throughout evolution, many different factors have been responsible for our development.

Everything from our geological position, surrounding species, and the weather have played a huge part in how we now function and think.

However, a lot has changed since then, and that is not something to ignore.

Today a big part of what forms our way of thinking stems from our childhood.

Ever since our birth, we learn through repetition, and this is precisely how habits are formed and strengthened.

In this chapter I'll explain in detail everything about them - from how they started to how to make them work in our favor.

So, What Are Habits?
- Definition

A habit is a learned behavior or sequence that has become reflexive overtime and therefore does not need a conscious command or intent.

What's important about habits is that they are learned through time and can be made into completely automatic processes.

However, maybe their most distinctive feature is that they're mainly dependent on previous repetition, and that's why doing them often, is the easiest way to make them a part of our brain.

- Origin

The part of our brain that's active when we're doing something out of habit is called the basal ganglia.

It's interesting to note that this is not the same part responsible for decision-making (the prefrontal cortex).

Within the basal ganglia of the brain, there are two different pathways through which we reach our habits- associative and automatic.

The associative pathway is connected to actions leading to food, warmth, shelter etc. - it's basically everything from habits to instincts.

The automatic pathway is where often repeated actions are stored like brushing teeth, putting on shoes etc. - this is for the habits we learn through repetition and positive reinforcement.
- Neurological loop

This is the most basic explanation of how habits are formed, and it consists of three steps - a cue, a routine, and a reward.

The cue is the trigger for the behavior itself, and it's mainly connected with location, time, previous action, or emotion.

Think of it like walking past the bathroom in the morning and brushing your teeth - this can be because of your place in the apartment, the morning hour, the fact that you just got out of bed, or that you still feel sleepy and want to wake up.

Next is the routine - this is the initially conscious actions that turned into habits.

We can use drinking coffee as an example - a lot of people start drinking coffee because they're tired or bored at the beginning (completely aware of the reasons and their actions) and end up forming a habit out of it through repeating the same thought process every day.

The final thing is the reward - this is pretty self-explanatory.

Habits are easily made through because of the rewarding feeling afterward.

For example, when you cook for yourself every night, you receive some free time throughout the next day and make this into a habit.

Why They Matter So Much

- Healthier life

Taking your meds, exercising, keeping a healthy diet and regular sleep schedule are all thanks to the formation of habits.

Positive actions and thoughts tend to avalanche and the same is true for repeating behavior - once you start it's much easier to keep going and this leads to a better physical and mental state.

Healthy habits also lead to a better perspective on life - once you start taking care of your body, it's much easier to boost your confidence and start working on your goals.

It's also worth mentioning that habits improve your day-to-day life because they're essentially little boosts of serotonin, which are always welcome.

- More brainpower

From an evolutionary standpoint, this is why habits were formed.

When you do something automatically you can keep your active focus on something else and still be successful in both.

By forming the habits you need and want, you will have the energy to achieve more complicated actions.

It's also important to mention that they save up time - once you've turned habits into automatic processes, you can do two or more things at the same time without it being detrimental to the results.

So, Think Of It This Way

Habits have been a part of our brain processes forever and for a good reason.

They help with survival, and they make many actions less taxing on the brain.

Habits also promote a healthier lifestyle and an easier and more enjoyable experience both from day to day and long term.

In the next chapter, I'll explain how to improve the habits we already have, get rid of negative ones and even build some we've always wanted to.

Stay tuned!

Notes:

5 HABITS THAT LEAD TO UNLIMITED SUCCESS

Revealing the top five habits that lead to unlimited success & how to build them into your daily routine…

Before we begin let me tell you why this is going to be a BIG read for you and why you may want to bookmark and refer to it over and over…

First, this is NOT some cooked-up fantasy, or (simply put) phony-baloney!

This information is a 'direct result' of a deep study of the works of the most prominent masters in the personal development realm from the 20th and 21st centuries.

Secondly, it's not some lecture in psychology either!

And, dispensing with all the formalities, I'll be getting straight to the point… Bringing to you the FIVE habits that you can pick to gain unlimited success in life…

Now you see what a terrific ride it's going to be?

Get ready and buckle up!

So, What Exactly Are Habits?
In simple terms habits are repetitive behavioral patterns... Cycles of thoughts and emotions in the mind that lead you to act.
It wouldn't be wrong to say that the mind is just a bundle of those repetitive patterns of thoughts...
James Allen, pioneer in the self-help movement, went so far as to say 'You Are What You Think' - therefore, your habits are you. Your thoughts are you...
And that pretty much explains why poor habits result in a poor YOU. And why certain good habits will turn you into your better - more successful, accomplished and balanced self.
It's time to get down to the *five success habits* as revealed by the gurus themselves!

1)Taking Responsibility

Yes! If you want to be successful start by being responsible for yourself! That might seem like hackneyed advice but to be honest 'it's gold'.

What happens is, by taking responsibility for yourself and everything you do, you establish yourself as the sovereign captain of your life's journey...

Suddenly your destiny is in your hands!

One common habit that Napoleon Hill, author of Think and Grow Rich, found in the world's most successful men was that they always took responsibility no matter what, and that leads them to grow.

So, you'd better start taking responsibility, because the gloomy path of blame-game leads to nowhere!

Do This: keep reinforcing in your head that your life is your responsibility, and never let your mind blame anyone. In some time you'll begin to experience freedom!

2)Action over Thinking!

Do you think too much? Many people think that 'thinking' is good and some even go to the extent of encouraging unnecessary imagination.

The truth is this: thought without action is not worth a dime!

Because, after all, this is a universe of activity (constant motion) and unless your thoughts set you into motion what good are they?

Thinking, without any definite action, is simply daydreaming or what else is it, you tell me?

Earl Nightingale, a legendary American speaker, stressed enough the fact that ideas are worthless unless we act upon them.

The bottom line is you've got to become action-oriented to be successful in life…

Do This: Set definite goals for yourself, and take definite actions to achieve them. Mark your progress every day. Make this into a habit!

3) Facing Challenges...

This means facing your fears! Everyone has fears and there's nothing wrong with that because as long as we're living we'll fear one thing or another.

Fears are not bad (unless neurotic), in fact one big difference between those who succeed in life and those who never *make it there* is,

- The former turn their fears into a driving force and pull through

- The latter let their fears take them over and take them down the drain.

The choice is yours...

If you've made the obvious choice then...

Do This: Set targets and push yourself out of your comfort zone every day. Meditate, and see yourself as fearless. With continuous practice you'll see the results!

4) Knowing the Value of Time
Have you ever heard the phrase, 'Time is Money'? Well, that's damn true!
Stephen Covey, a renowned American speaker, believed and insisted on the value of time so much so that he even drew up a Time Management Matrix for people to use and spend their time most efficiently.
Among Covey's bestselling '7 Habits of Highly Effective People' he placed time management at number 3 - which goes to show what time meant to him.
So, how to be effective with time?
Do This:
- Set your priorities right…
- Stop overthinking (because that eats up time, isn't it?)
- Be quick and active (taking good care of your health so laziness won't kick in)
- Start respecting time in its true sense and 'realize' that it is your LEASE ON LIFE.
The last one must really JOLT you!

5) Honesty is the Best Policy!

Sir Edwin Sandys was quite right when he uttered those historic words…
You don't need a lecture on honesty, do you?
That 'honesty' is the essence of all of the world's religions, of all scriptures and that he who's honest will lead a content life… is known to all!
The big issue with honesty is that, the majority of the time, when we have a choice between the truth and lie we go with the lie. Because being honest never looks very promising at first glance to most of us!
Why? What's the root of that?
This: We're short-term people, with a short-sighted attitude to life…
If you want to lead a successful and fully content life (in the long-term) with a light and happy heart - make honesty an inseparable part of you!
No **'Do This'** this time, because you know how to be honest and true. There's no practice.

5) Help Yourself Before Others – Why It is Important

Do you find it hard to say no to people? Have you ever said yes to someone even when it was inconvenient or to your detriment?

Maybe you find it hard to say no to others because you are afraid of being called selfish and self-serving.

Many people struggle with this, and while it is great to be known as the go-to and reliable person, it is also a great responsibility.

Yes, it is necessary to help others but not when it is at a disadvantage to you.

You will always be needed by others, friends, family, coworkers, etc. but remember that you're also needed by... You.

When you are not in the right space mentally and physically, there's no way you can impart someone positively.

Now let us discuss this intricate topic a little further …

Importance of Putting Yourself First

We can only give what we possess, and loving oneself before others is a pathway to fulfillment and happiness.

When you prioritize yourself, you automatically multiply that, which you are able to give others, whether it is spiritual, emotional or material.

And here's why that's important...

Surely you want to give the best to your loved ones, and they want the same for you.

Spending so much time loving others and not yourself could lead to resentment, especially when you are not getting the same energy back.

Carving out time to care for yourself improves self-worth, which translates into happiness and a feeling of fulfillment.

People will treat you how you treat yourself, so if you place yourself last, they will do the same thing.

If you say yes at all times, they will take you for granted, so be kind but not a pushover.

By putting a greater focus on yourself, confidence also improves and you then go on to become more respected.

Striving to please everyone around you can get exhausting and this strains all aspects of life, especially your relationships.

Remember to focus more on yourself and ensure you are in great shape before taking care of others.

Once your energy is revived, you have more to offer to those around you, and you will see your relationships with them get better.

Disregarding your own needs for others can leave you stressed, exhausted, and overwhelmed which can take a toll on your health.

Stress is in fact, one of the biggest dangers for your health, due to its innate ability to buffer your body's immune function and growth.

You NEED your body to be relaxed and strong enough for all your activities and if you don't find the time to rest, your body will do it for you and leave you sick.

How to Put Yourself First
There is a fine line between prioritizing yourself in a productive way and being overly selfish.
To get others to love and respect you, you need to occupy the number 1 position in your own life… In the right way.
Here's how to do that.

Boundaries are necessary, and if you fail to do this, you start living for others.
This doesn't mean completely discarding other people's feelings, but rather, learning to find the right balance.
Learn to say no, and let go of the fear that people would stop loving you because it is not true.

Doing what you love is the greatest form of self-care and it's time to start making this a priority.
The more you do this, the more your self-care routine improves and the happier you become.

Being around people that inspire you will help you develop those traits you admire in them.
This elevates your energy instead of depleting it because you are challenged to become a better person.

A major part of caring for your body is paying attention to what goes inside it.
Nutrition is the fuel of the body and it should be used to optimize functions, health and well-being
Focus on whole food sources that are nutrient dense and avoid any highly processed foods and packed products.

Final Thoughts

Helping yourself first is not selfish, it is the responsible and right thing to do. Not only will it improve your well-being, but it will also make you a better person for those around you.

Love those around you but remember that you come first, because you are that fountain for the love you give to others!

This page purposely left blank for your notes

HOW DOES APPEARANCE AFFECT YOUR
Self-Esteem?

You've heard the phrase "Appearances can be deceiving", right? Not only is that absolutely true, but it can also have a big influence on your self-esteem.

Self-esteem is linked with self-confidence which, like most things, is set to be formed by how the outside world sees us.

This does not mean that the way you feel is dictated by what people think of you, but on some level, it really does make a difference.

What is self-esteem, and how does it develop?

Self-esteem is the value and worth we subjectively evaluate ourselves with as a whole. With this definition, we can easily say that the part of ours that we evaluate the hardest is our body image.

It is linked with how we perceive the world and how we think the world perceives us. This means that every little thing that we do regarding boosting our self-esteem is to better our approach to different situations in life.

It's important to remember that people are not born with any gained level of self-esteem. It's something that develops with time as a result of our upbringing and social contacts.

A thing that can affect our body image and self-esteem is being raised in an abusive environment, physically or mentally, or being born with a distinct disfigurement or some kind of visible difference from others.

The early years

If a person is subjected to different types of public or domestic psychological or physical assault, it most probably will affect one's self-esteem.

Even small things like a kid in preschool or kindergarten making fun of another can cause doubt in that young mind.

Our surroundings and the opinion of our social circle, even If we think we don't get bothered by it, play a huge role in establishing healthy confidence in us.

If a person starts to acknowledge a flaw in the way you look, it is likely that you will start questioning your appearance.

That's the way we are built, and even if we sometimes say we don't care about what people think of us, we still soak in that remark.

If we give in to the idea that society and people form the way we feel about ourselves, we have a much harder time accepting who we are and what we look like in a healthy concept.

On the other hand, If we listened to family and friends that wanted to help us when the doubt was only forming, there is a pretty big chance we would know how to handle this kind of dismissive behavior towards us better.

What our appearance says about us

The way we perceive ourselves is the way we want the world to see us. It's as simple as that.

We go the extra mile to have a more pleasant effect when we look at ourselves in the mirror most of the time.

But in reality, the thing that matters most for building steady self-esteem is accepting that **we are what we are, and we're perfect like this.**

It's easier said than done, but it's a simple philosophy to live your life without the stress and pressure of social evaluation.

Things like comparing yourself to other people or not quite seeing your good sides can be dealt with and should be.

Recognizing your own qualities, talents, and abilities is the way to build a stronger relationship with yourself and create stable self-esteem and self-confidence.

HOW TO CHALLENGE YOURSELF?

Imagine this – you are at a certain age where you face tough decisions, have to let go of some past things that have cradled you until now and you're not sure what to do.

Having to face difficult decisions, having to grow as a person and withstand what life has installed for you – well, better learn how to challenge yourself, before It gets late.

This doesn't mean that there is a right or wrong time to start challenging yourself, but the sooner you begin, the better.

What exactly does that mean?
To challenge yourself is to jump out of the barriers you have created for yourself, to escape your comfort zone, and to grow as a person.
Many people don't realize how much this could benefit the improvement in their lifestyle.
To challenge oneself to grow as a person is something all of us should be keen on doing as much as possible.
There is no bad timing or wrong place to start.
For a person to take the extra step and force him/herself to do things that he, or she, wouldn't be caught dead doing before, is the thing that keeps the drive in us.
The thing that gets us from this stage in our life to the other.

Okay, But How Do I Do That?
There really is no concrete game plan when it comes to jumping your own boundaries. It is, as it should be, a very intimate course of action.
A person should first know his/her weaknesses, as well as good sides, in order to start challenging themselves.
Nevertheless, there are some universal methods that are, more or less, suitable for everyone to try.
Even though our personal growth is substantially our job and responsibility, it's nice to hear out some professional opinions.

Let's start at the beginning

The first, and most important, thing to start with is focusing on a goal.

This could be any goal, don't think big or small, just one that gets us started.

The reason why we need this is, that focusing on something that gets the blood pumping is crucial for the first kick in the bum.

Things like starting a new book and sticking to it, or visiting a new museum every Saturday, could help with the process.

Do you know how much you sleep?

A key asset to the "new you" is changing your daily routines, starting with one of the biggies – sleep.

I bet you don't follow how many hours a week you sleep and it's a changing number, I know.

Well, how about you set an alarm for a certain hour for every night of the week and get up at a certain time every morning.

If you don't think this will change anything you are mistaken.

Sticking to a regular sleep schedule not only benefits your health but will also teach you discipline and build your character.

Technology who?

Believe me, you will be just fine If you let go of your technological device for just a day. That's all that It takes – one day.

By doing so you help your brain and body to develop a new and steady connection to the world around you without the help, or distractions, of your phone, laptop, TV, etc.

After all, technology is fairly unnatural for humans - We were not designed to sit in front of a screen all day.

The body was made to run, crawl, climb, jump, sprint, swim, and dive - All of these activities, with the absence of an internet connection, will allow you to develop a true mind-body-world connection, that is much more precious and beneficial than any piece of tech.

Growing as a person
As time goes by you will push yourself easier and easier and will start to crave more of It. This is a perfect time to start learning new languages, new cultures.
Maybe take a class, or two.
Or maybe, you can even invest in something you care about and believe in. Just remember that challenging yourself doesn't stop with the boundaries the world creates, it stops with the boundaries you create.

Take-Home Message
We live in a world of comfort that is more and more oriented towards making everything as easy and automated as possible.

This is the precise reason why you should consider setting yourself challenges.

Challenge yourself mentally.

Challenge yourself physically.

Challenge yourself spiritually.

Challenge brings about positive change.

HOW TO EAT ON A BUSY SCHEDULE

Many of us are trapped in the busy city life, where time is tight, everything is rushed and there is little to no time for you to give your body all the essential nutrients it needs.

Without a doubt, daily life-induced stress, combined with malnutrition can lead to a serious downfall in performance, both mental and physical.

This daily life-induced stress inevitably leads to burnouts and one of the best steps to deal with it, is to learn how to fuel your body on a day to day basis.

Is Nutrition Really Everything?

Now, nutrition isn't really everything there is to managing stress from daily life, but it can be a powerful tool to do so for a couple of reasons.

First off, food is not just nutrients.

Though the common belief about food nowadays is mainly related to the caloric and macronutrient content, that is not all there is to nutrition.

Besides being the body's fuel for performance and recovery, nutrition is a form of art, enjoyment and pleasure.

This can bring about a more relaxed, content state of mind which will have a positive impact on your perception of daily-life stress.

So how can you take care of your nutrition consistently, without having to spend countless hours in the kitchen, or all your money on ordered food?

Check out some good tips below, as I give you some insight on easy, seamless, efficient meal-prep you can use on a busy schedule!

#1 Pick Food Sources

Nutrition isn't all that hard and its main purpose is to give the body all the essential nutrient it needs to sustain optimal functioning of all bodily systems and processes.

The two essential nutrients for the body are protein and fats, as they play major roles in all internal processes.

Besides protein and fats, you have carbohydrates, which are not essential, but good to consume, especially if you are mentally and physically active.

Here are my best picks for whole foods, which you can place at the core of your daily menu:
- Beef
- Pork
- Dairy products
- Eggs
- Sweet potatoes
- Normal potatoes
- White/brown rice
- Broccoli
- Carrots
- Kiwis
- Bananas
- Mangoes
- Coconuts
- Oats

#2 Cook in bulk!

If you are looking to save as much time as possible and be efficient with your nutrition and food budget, cooking your own food is your best bet.

Furthermore, to catch up with a busy schedule, you have to think ahead of time and prepare your food for the next couple of days.

Preparing your main products in bigger amounts (meats, grains and potatoes) is your best bet, and you can then use those as core products for different meals, where you add side foods such as vegetables, sauces and other side products which can enrich the meal.

#3 Pack It Up!

Once you've established the core products of your daily menu and cooked them, all you have to do is pack them up and put them in the fridge for later use.

Whenever you're going out and about, all you need to do is take a food box with you and then, you can consume that any time, anywhere, without having to order food.

Home-cooked food is the best and least expensive option!

Don't Forget Though

In the beginning, preparing your own food may seem time-consuming, especially if you are not used to cooking.

However, once you establish a concrete system, cooking all your food for the week will take just a couple of cooking sessions.

This in turn will save you time, money and on top of that, will allow you to consistently provide your body with all the essential nutrients that it needs.

And so, are you ready to make a change for the better?

How To Effectively Manage Your Time & Productivity

Struggling with time management lately? You are not alone. Most people routinely feel stressed for not being productive the way they are supposed to be.

The good news is that you can prevent this stress by using time management strategies to become more efficient.

Why use those strategies? Well, it is quite simple - Time is your most valuable asset and so, you don't really want to waste it.

So without further ado, let me take you through 10 time management tips and tricks you can put to use in your life!

Laura Vanderkam, who's a career development writer, suggests that individuals have more willpower in the early morning than the rest of the day regardless of whether they are a morning person or night person.

Following this idea, you can utilize the time in the morning to do more productive things, such as reading, training, planning , and making decisions accordingly with a fresh mind.

"But… I'm not really a morning person, I feel like I've been beaten with a bat as soon as I wake up!"

If that's the case, you can develop the habit of waking up early gradually if you are not a morning person.

Keeping a diary is perhaps one of the best things you can do in the context of monitoring your routine activities and the results that come from them.

This simple habit will enable you to define your goals, express yourself and even reflect on past actions, as well as record your progress.

In keeping a diary like this, you'll have the chance to see everything pen on paper and will get a better idea of the time that certain tasks consume and the results that they yield.

Time management expert, Dave Crenshaw in his book *The Myth of Multitasking: How "Doing It All" Gets Nothing Done* says that: "When someone tells me that they are good at multitasking, I know they're inefficient. Saying that you're a good multitasker is the same as saying that you're good at using a less effective method to get things done."

And whether you want to believe it or not, this might just turn out to be the exact truth for most people.

Focus your undivided attention on the task at hand, to get it as quickly and efficiently done, as possible.

Ultradian rhythms term is defined as the natural rhythms that the body cycles through every 90-120 minutes.

This term was coined by Peretz Lavie and it promotes the idea that you should work when your energy levels are high and rest when you feel tired.

If you want to boost your productivity consider following your ultradian rhythms and avoid working when your body and mind only offer resistance to that work.

Phones have controlled our professional and personal lives ever since the first smartphone was introduced to the world.

And though phones can make us anxious and even depressed, they can also be a very effective tool to boost productivity when used correctly.

To fully focus, start by removing instant stimuli from your main screen and concentrating on the important tasks.

Use the applications that actually help your work process and avoid diving into those news feed scrolling sessions.

Remember that the phone is just a tool and if you don't use it correctly, you might smash your nail (metaphorically).

Speaking of phones, the best way to be productive through phones is to install productivity applications.

There are various applications that you can use - one of them is Focus@Will

Apps like Focus@Will allow you to stay on the right track by removing all the distractions.

Look out for those apps and find the one that suits you best!

Just like mindfulness, meditation is a mental exercise, capable of bringing realizations of many things, including unconscious actions of yours that rob you of time.

Besides that, meditation may help you clear your mind and bring about a better focus, thus allowing you to manage your actions and time more effectively.

People who meditate regularly are able to avoid distractions and focus on important tasks.

The best thing? Meditation can massively help you manage stress and even overcome procrastination.

So hey, don't forget to pay some attention to your inner world.

Being one of the strongest mental and physical stimulants, caffeine can be the thing that makes or breaks your productivity.

The right amount of caffeine can increase mental focus and output, but too much can make you feel anxious.

So really, analyze your coffee intake and judge it objectively - Is it helping you or is it burning you out?

If the latter is true, then consider using caffeine only in moments when you need it (i.e when you are tired or just need a kickstart).

Ultimately, aim for no more than 2 cups a day, as that will provide a healthy amount of caffeine, to promote focus and mental output, without leading to a caffeine crash or any other undesired side effects caused by excessive consumption of caffeine.

Did you know that personalities like Da Vinci and Einstein adored power naps in the afternoon?

The reason why power naps work is because they allow you to deprive the senses of information and thus, get into a more relaxed, playful state of mind.

Additionally, the fact that you're not processing something from the outside allows your body and mind to get a brief, powerful energy rejuvenation.

Ever felt the energy from a quality sleep session? Well, the power nap is the same, but on a smaller scale, so do use that, but be careful not to fall asleep!

Overcommitting can always affect your productivity and oftentimes, it can rob you of your own time.

As per *Psychology Today,* the extreme desire to please everyone and always say yes comes from our intrinsic fear of causing clash, dissatisfaction or upset by declining to help those around us.

This is why you should learn the art of saying no and be your best productive self, despite anything else!

Final Thoughts

In a dynamic world like ours, the effective management of time and effort is something to really pay attention to, as you may easily swerve towards a burnout, accompanied with a severe lack of time.

The secret to achieving balance is in analyzing yourself, your schedule and keeping good track of your habits, both in and outside of work, as well as your personal life.

At the end of the day, once you reach the point of balance, time management will be seamless.

Stay productive, stay efficient!

Notes:

BECOMING MORE ORGANIZED IN YOUR DAILY LIFE

Little Things That Help You Stay On Top Of Your Game

We've all had those days when our organizational skills seem to have just wandered off somewhere.

It's like they have decided to take a holiday, leaving us with just pieces of plans, which often makes us feel powerless.

These days are completely normal and happen to everyone from time to time.

After all, we can't always be perfect… Right?

However, if you have more trouble organizing your day-to-day life than you would like to, it may start hindering your overall experience and feelings.

If you're having trouble staying organized, keep reading as we provide valuable tips and tricks on becoming more structured, organized, and orderly in your day-to-day tasks!

So let's jump right into the topic with the first and most important tip!

#1 Give Yourself The Best

First things first - before you start working on the parts of yourself you want to improve, you have to make sure that you're covering all of your basic needs and desires.

Changing habits or making new ones is always tricky, and it can turn out to be almost impossible if you aren't providing your body with what it needs in the first place.

Things like getting enough sleep, eating healthy, and sustaining a proper balance between work and social life may seem like they don't have a lot in common with improving your organizational skills, but that's not true.

If you have all of your basic needs covered you will be able to focus on your more complicated aspirations.

This is the only way to ensure that you will have the energy you need to improve and actually start working.

Start from yourself.

#2 Write Everything Down

Next up, we suggest you keep a journal where you write down your responsibilities, ideas, and even tasks you've completed

Having everything in one place makes it easier for you to keep track of your next move.

You can do this digitally or on paper. Both have their merits. A digital itinerary means that you can easily alter, add or remove events and their specifics.

However, if you have a more classical approach, writing everything down may be the better option for you.

It's worth noting here that writing everything down pen on paper does wonders for the brain.

If you have done it, you know that it brings a sense of peacefulness when you see your plans written down in your own handwriting.

Even more so, some people find the action of writing itself incredibly therapeutic.

Regardless of which of the options you choose to go for, the core benefits of keeping a journal are the same - Everything is in one place, which makes forgetting something improbable, and allows you to structure your days more effortlessly.

#3 Reward Time

Another idea is to implement some sort of reward system for yourself. Things are best learned through positive reinforcement, so try and think of little ways to make yourself feel good when you manage to keep to your schedule.

For instance, every time you organize a part of your day or stick to a premade plan, you give yourself a small gift - it can be anything from enjoying a piece of chocolate to watching an episode of your favorite show.

Another option, if there's something you've wanted to do for a long time, is to give yourself a point after each achievement - gather enough points, and you receive the reward.

It can be something like purchasing a new phone or traveling somewhere for a few days - pretty much any big thing you know you'd enjoy but also want to feel like you've earned it.

Through this method, you can start teaching your mind that organization is a positive instead of a tedious concept and that if you follow your own rules and are consistent about them, you can achieve whatever you want to.

#4 Share With Loved Ones

Finally, you can start sharing your adventures with friends and family.

After you're sure that you've made a positive change and are more organized, you can start sharing your newly learned skills with other people.

Make some plans together or maybe even be the one responsible for organizing a bunch of your friends.

Most things are more fun if you involve the ones you love, and by being organized, you can do so with ease.

Taking the initiative and planning something for you and the people you're close to is a surefire way to show your appreciation for them and maybe even surprise them with a plan for something you both have been dying to do.

As a bonus, organizing something like this yourself assures you that your hard work was worth it, making you even more confident in the future.

Final Thoughts

Organizational skills are essential regardless of what your job and social life are.

Being able to rely solely on yourself for your plans gives you freedom as nothing else does.

Being a good organizer also boosts your self-esteem.

Not to mention, the opinion others have of you will surely benefit from this change, too!

Maybe the best part of having good organizational skills is that you will be able to fill your days to the brim with things you love to do.

So… Start. Now!

Notes:

HOW TO MAKE YOUR MIND WORK FOR YOU

A perfect four-step guide for you to put a leash on your restless mind and make it obey YOU!

There are lots of 'mind control' workshops out there and it seems like everyone has become an expert on the subject of the mind these days.

At the workshop an enthusiastic speaker will present you with some ideas, charge you up with his talk, get you to do some activity and by the end of the session you already feel like the conqueror of the world.

What next? Back home, the enthusiasm he pumped you up with is slowly oozing out...

And, before you know it you're back at square one.

The thing is that NOT everyone is a mind expert and, sadly, the majority are just doing business.

To take control of your mind - you'll have to look at your mind YOURSELF!

So, let's get ready to first understand what's the mind...

The Mystique of Mind

The mind doesn't exist on its own! It lives on thoughts… Without thoughts there can be no mind. That's the reason why in deep sleep when there are no thoughts there is no mind.

So, running after the mind is pointless because you're chasing an illusion. What exists is the thought. Therefore… 'We've got to work upon thought!'

That brings us to the question: what's thought?

Well, thoughts are made up of the neuron patterns in the brain which carry the sum of all our memories. They keep spinning energy frequencies in the brain non-stop and these energy forms are experienced by us as thoughts or thinking.

That brings us down to one final question:

'How to get your brain to operate at higher frequencies so that it'll produce the thinking that'll work FOR you?'

The answer to the big question lies in the four steps below…

1) Take a Holistic Approach

This universe is a single unit - and today, there's enough evidence to back that… There's no individuality in reality because everything is dependent on one thing or another for survival.

The realization that 'everything around you is part of you' will shatter your limited thinking to pieces and you'll start taking a holistic approach toward life…

Because you'll then see that everything around you affects the frequency on which your brain works.

For example, everything you eat, your daily activities, your friends' circle, etc. all of that determines what type of thoughts your brain will produce.

And those thoughts will spur you into action.

So…

For the Body:

- Stay on top of your health
- Best diet - organic food, NO junk
- Daily workout

For the Surroundings:

- Spend time in nature
- Surround yourself with whatever 'elevates' you
- Befriend positive people
- Avoid energy suckers

2) Rewire Your Thought!

Thought is responsible for all your actions and reactions, it's what makes you successful and what makes you a failure.

Thought is the source of your life, but if you try and catch it you'll end up in misery. Because you can never touch energy in its subtlest form.

The only thing you can and MUST do is raise the frequency of your brain so it produces the right kind of thoughts.

To achieve that you must realize the difference between imagination and reality, because a mind that can't differentiate between reality and fiction will always 'misbehave.'

That's why in spirituality they say when the veil of illusions falls off your mind and you see the reality - you become enlightened.

To bring your mind back to reality you do the following...

Affirmations (Best before sleep):
- I'm a part of the Universe (Everything works together, YOU are NOT alone in this universe)
- I'm Fearless (Fear is only an emotion that we create)
- Limitless Possibilities

Study Spiritual Stuff:
- The Bible (Book of Psalms)
- The Power of Now (Eckhart Tolle)
- Inner Engineering (Sadhguru)
- From Bondage to Freedom (Osho)
- Poetry of Rumi

Meditation:
- Getting to know the Creator of ALL things (God)
- Focus on a particular object
- Practicing surrender

There are innumerable affirmations, books or meditation practices and you can choose the ones that best suit you! See what's best for you and then STICK TO IT!

3)Questioning Your Worries

FACT: In the United States alone 40 million adults suffer from some kind of anxiety!

A mind that is in a state of constant worry and stress will never be able to function at its peak. Because it's always caught in anxiety and working through the fight or flight mode (defensive) it can never create something positive.

Get this straight: Your mind will only work FOR you when it's absolutely free of the shackles of worry!

The best way to get free of your worries is by questioning their reality.

Do this: take a piece of paper and pen down all your worrisome thoughts on it... Write in as much detail as possible. Now fully analyze each thought. Crack the patterns in your thoughts. Test them against reality.

With continuous practice you'll get rid of worry! Because you'll see that *most of your worries are just fantasies with no truth to them...*

This method is called Cognitive Behavioral Therapy(CBT) in psychology.

Google the best CBT methods yourself and start right away.

4) Sit in Silence

The mind is always restless (chattering) and that's the reason why you're not able to focus!

To achieve control over the mind you'll have to quiet it up, but you can't force it to be quiet. Using force will do the opposite and it'll create further restlessness.

The way to control the mind is not 'doing' but 'non-doing.'

Do nothing! Just sit in silence for ten minutes every day. Drop everything on the level of your mind and JUST BE!

This is a wonderful practice and can do you wonders...

Implement Right Now!
A trick your mind will now play upon you is stalling - don't fall for that!
The four steps you've read up there can change your life…
Use them to make up your own plan and get started NOW before you fall prey to procrastination!

Notes:

HOW TO SET CORRECT GOALS FOR YOURSELF

Many people fall into the cycle of setting goals that they never complete.
This could be because they have no idea what they want, or in other cases, don't know how to attain their targets.
A wrong approach towards goal setting is a major cause of these challenges.
Whatever you set out to achieve, it is necessary to know how to set the right goals and pave your way there.
In this chapter, I will help you learn the importance of creating goals, and more importantly how to set correct goals for YOURSELF.

The Importance of Goal Setting

Effective goal setting is a crucial step in shaping your desired future and developing the motivation and discipline to put in the actual work.

Here's why goal setting is important.

- **It Improves Focus**

Goals help to present a clear picture of your plans and enable you to focus on the important aspects of your journey.

Without goals, you lose direction and so, goal setting may help you recognize the areas you need to improve on and determine the actions and path needed to bring you closer to your aim.

- **It helps you track progress**

To measure how much success you have attained, you need to set well-defined goals.

It is easy to get discouraged when you feel you have not achieved enough, but tracking progress makes you notice those little strides which is a confidence booster.

Goals are practically an approximation of the end result caused by your action, so tracking your actual results opposed to your goals, is important!

- **It Curbs Procrastination**

A clearly envisioned goal gives you an inner drive to actually get up and do what has to be done.

Those clear goals will keep you accountable and motivated to get things done at the appropriate time.

Without a doubt, goal-setting is a great way to beat procrastination for the better, so make use of it!

How to Set Correct Goals and Achieve Them

To realize your goals, you need to know how to set them. Take a look at the following steps to aid you in the process.

- **Determine your vision**

Your vision is the final destination and goals are the steps that take you there.

If you pursue too many goals at the same time, you might not achieve any significant final end result, because you're trying to be the jack of all trades!

So, before setting that goal, determine if it is something you want and would be willing to commit to.

- **Create SMART goals**

Once you have streamlined your purpose, make sure your goals fit into the SMART criteria. In essence, your goals should be;

- **S**pecific

They must be clear and precise, you should know the why, when, how, and who of all your goals. Generalized goals are a recipe for failure.

Notes:

How to use the Pomodoro technique?

Let's face it - we're human and can't work like robots. It's just not possible to be a fully functional working machine that doesn't rest and can be 100% productive all time.

So how do we tackle that? How do we cope with the exhaustion from working? Whether It's on your studies, a project, work-related or just doing the bills?

Maybe the answer is right under our noses, perhaps it's been there the whole time, and we haven't paid attention to it.

Or maybe the answer is a plain old tomato…

What is the Pomodoro technique?

The Pomodoro technique is a time-related plan that helps you be more productive and energy-efficient.

Its creator's name is Francesco Cirillo and when he was a student, he decided to end his struggles with his studies by setting a timer for 25 minutes and then taking a break for 5 minutes.

The word "Pomodoro" is Italian for tomato, and in Cirillo's case, the timer that he used was in the shape of a tomato.

The method turned out so effective Cirillo wrote a 130-page book on the topic.

Waste time to save time!

The genius of the technique is in its simplicity. When we need to be focused and decide to power through a project, our brain starts to wonder after 30 minutes or so.

Instead of constantly finding ways to occupy yourself with everything but not the project why not just plan to waste time…?

Think of it as an award for the last half an hour that you read, wrote, etc., and take those sweet five minutes to reload and unwind your mind.

It's estimated that this can boost your attention span and increase your productivity up to 40%.

Not to mention that it leaves you more fulfilled with the work you managed to check off your itinerary.

So, how does It work and how to use it

The idea behind the technique is really simple, and you have to follow these steps:

<u>Get a sheet of paper and a timer</u> for starters. You need to write down all the things you have to be done with and focus on them one at a time.

This is important because you need to bother yourself with only one thing at a time so as not to preoccupy your brain activity and start to slouch.

<u>Don't cheat the timer.</u> The timer should be set for 25 minutes in which you stay focused and that is it, no more, no less.

If you want the method to work, you need to let the timer do its work and focus on your task without any interruptions — especially the ones that include messaging someone or returning emails.

<u>Write down your progress.</u>

After you're finished with your work session, put the 5-minute break mark on your timer and write down one Pomodoro on the sheet of paper.

Then you can record what you've done until now and let your brain rest. It's really important not to spend those five minutes browsing the net or looking at your phone.

Just relax and rest up for the next 25 minutes.

<u>Patience is a virtue,</u> especially If you follow the plan as instructed.

After you've got four pomodoros written down, you can take a longer break of 15-30 minutes. This is key for pumping up your stimulation and widening your efficiency span.

In these extra minutes, you can do some squats, or push-ups, just to get your body to feel more active than static. Also, light snacks that are good for brain activity, like nuts, are also recommended.

After a while, you will see how these small things become a part of your work routine, and you get better and better results the more you practice this technique.

To Wrap It Up...

Managing energy and productivity may be a hard task, especially with the amount of information we're bombarded with in the modern-day world.

If you are finding it hard to keep your attention span and focus on point, do give this technique a shot!

IMPROVING YOUR
QUALITY OF LIFE

Part One

Living a quality life is about finding a way to turn things around when life gets difficult. It includes turning fear to peace, blame to remorse, diversion to clarity, and times when we can be thankful for everything right, particularly when too much seems to be wrong.

When things are difficult, it's normal to lament or be fearful and we may make mistakes that we could later come to regret.

When we get off track, though, I believe the key to living a good life is figuring out how to get back on track, through the doubts and fear.

These nine questions will assist you in making positive changes in your life and improve the quality of your life if you remain persistent with them.

We can get so wrapped up in the affairs of life that we forget who we truly are. That said, we each have something special about us that no one else has. This worth stems solely from the fact that you are who you are and it has nothing to do with your achievements.

Ask yourself this; who are you when no one else is around? That you left alone with nothing but their thoughts? Essentially, it's the best version of you when you're being true to yourself, bound to your inner highest self, and not giving a damn about what other people think. What does your energy look like, and how does it feel to be you?

Once you get in touch with your inner energy and figure out what makes you on point, interact with this force, embrace it, and let it shine to the world.

Life is easier when you have a sense of purpose. Even at the end of someone's life, research has shown that having a project that gives you a sense of meaning gives you the feeling of happiness and content.

It keeps you occupied and engaged as well with the bigger picture grounding your focus on the most important things. According to one study, people over the age of 50 (with purposeful projects) had a longer life and feelings of content as the purpose impacted both their physical and mental health.

Last, do you have a plan for getting things back on track when things aren't going as smoothly as you'd like? In tough times, what makes you reach out, apologize, fix ties, or find something to be thankful for?

What makes you turn it around when you're on the verge of being irritable? What makes you change your perspective, reclaim your strength when you're feeling down, and choose to do good in the world and your own heart?

Improve your problem-solving skills and learn how you effectively fit in this world.

CONCLUSION
There's no easy formula to create a quality life, considering your loved ones too. It's always a work in progress and you don't want to loosen your grip once you start getting it right.

Other stuff to pay attention to include; working hard and smart, having an easy approach towards life, doing the stuff that makes you happy, fostering healthy relationships, standing for your principles, and sticking to your values. Having a "Backbone".

IMPROVING YOUR
QUALITY OF LIFE

Part Two

"It is our decisions, not our conditions that determine our quality of life", says John C Maxwell.

Quality of life can be hard to define because its definition can vary by people's lifestyle and their preferences in life.

For some people it might be, becoming CEO of a well-known company, for others, it might be just fulfilling their wanderlust in the Amazon Forest.

Either way, quality of life is a subjective and intangible term that is the outcome of one's decisions and wishful choices.

People who were born in rough conditions are not at fault but if their deathbed is laid under the same roof then it is their choice of living.

As Jack Canfield once said, "There is only one person responsible for the quality of life you live and that person is you." Therefore, one can certainly improve their quality of life by making the right decisions whether it be financial or social.

Improving Your Quality of Life
Improving the quality of life is not a hard nut to crack and there are certain aspects to pay more attention to and certain things to do that may help you increase your overall life quality.
Let's have a look at some of them.

Be Grateful for What You Have
It's human nature to envy what others have and we lack - whether it be good grades, lifelong friendships, flourishing careers, flaunting pay, or a loving soulmate.
We sometimes drain our entire energy over such a lost cause while instead, we should be spending that energy in celebrating what we have.
Being grateful for little things in life can help us to live a happier and contented life.

Maintain Healthy Relationships

The most important factor required to have a better quality of life is to maintain healthy relationships whether it be with your life partner, friends, or parents and siblings.

Research has indicated a high correlation of increased happiness, life satisfaction, psychological well-being, and reduced suicide risk with having a healthy relationship.

Abusive relationships and toxic friendships can reduce one's intention to live further and may lead to depression and hopelessness.

Therefore, try to maintain healthy relationships and let go of the toxic ones.

Find Meaning in Your Work

Is pay the most relevant factor for opting a job opportunity? Many people subconsciously agree to this notion because they link higher pay to being able to afford a better standard of living.

But a better standard of living is no way near to having a better quality of life. Being part of a working environment that is meaningless and directionless can lead to harmful consequences, it can emotionally and physically drain one person and reduce the quality of life to an alarming point.

Hence, choose a job that might not pay well but might help you to stay well.

ME Time

The age of 22-30, where we feel so much pressurized by the expectations that society holds for us. Getting degrees with distinctions, getting well-paying jobs, getting great life partners, having healthy children and what not!

So much to achieve in such a short span that we actually forget to take our time for ourselves.

Research has proved that people who take their free time for themselves tend to have lesser stresses, improved moods, and have enhanced problem-solving skills.

Therefore, always try to have little Me time before going to bed.

Be Optimistic

Optimism refers to being able to always find the positive side of most unpleasant situations. That seems impossible for extreme situations such as departing a loved one but this is an actual test of life to get yourself out of adversity by being optimistic.

In the pursuit of getting a better quality of life one must hop on the bandwagon of optimism and envision the best possible outcome.

Stay Healthy

The three rituals of staying healthy include a good night's sleep, a healthy balanced diet, and exercise.

All three drivers are extremely crucial to keep your life moving on the path of getting the best quality of life.

Missing on any one of them can cause detrimental effects on your health and can spare you from enjoying the moments of life.

Notes:

LEARNING TO TAKE YOUR FEELINGS INTO ACCOUNT

The Effect Of Social Media And How To Hear Your Own Voice In A Sea Of Others

There's a lot to be said about human emotion because, quite frankly, it is very complicated.

Many scientists believe that some of the fundamental differences we as a species have are because we feel certain emotions in specific ways.

The way we understand and experience love, anger, care, disappointment, or hope is crucial in formulating how we act in many situations and can change our futures in the blink of an eye.

This is why genuinely understanding our emotions is so important - by figuring out how different situations make us feel and where the roots of those feelings lie, we can understand how they govern us and potentially what we would like to change.

Social Media And Society's Opinion

We live in a time where feelings are simultaneously being broadcast and hidden which may sound like a paradox but is, in fact, very true!

Let's focus on social media - the center of attention for a big part of modern society.

At its core, this is a virtual space explicitly made so that people can share exactly how they feel in each moment.

Videos, photos, posts, tweets, comments, reactions - all of these are essentially forms of self-expression that allow us to convey our innermost desires, fears, opinions, and hopes.

A digital, eternal library of our human experience where everything is said, shared and stored.

This has its obvious positive sides - freedom of speech for one, is actively supported, which hasn't always been the case.

Creativity is encouraged and given its due credit, thus broadening all sorts of cultural knowledge and allowing all kinds of talents to be noticed and appreciated despite where they come from and what they are.

Forming an opinion and standing by it has also never been easier, which is tremendously beneficial because it focuses the individual's attention on their personal choices and the reasons behind them.

These things are all connected with emotions and have all had an impact due to the exponential growth of social media.

The Paradox

Now, this is where the paradox mentioned above comes into play.

For one, by having all of this information just a few clicks away, it's easy to feel overwhelmed or even discouraged to share your thoughts and ideas - after all, there's always going to be someone better than you.

Historically speaking, there hasn't been a time in which the previous statement was not true.

However, today we can find and keep our focus on each person who is superior in our eyes.

Sure the people who lived before the golden age of the internet also understood that they probably weren't the absolute best in their respective fields, but it's a different thing to realize this in theory and actually to see those people and their achievements every day.

This often takes a toll on our self-esteem and makes us disregard our feelings and thoughts.

The Aspects Of Social Media

With the above-said in mind, we would like to make another important mention here - just because you see it, doesn't mean it's the whole story!

Social media posts tend to be highly positive - unrealistically so.

It's natural for the creator only to want to share their finished product or their final thoughts, without mentioning all the hardship that came before that.

However, the viewer often forgets that this hardship was the central part of the narrative.

By seeing everyone elses lives through rose-colored glasses (or filters), we often end up judging ourselves because our worlds have different nuances and colors.

This can bring us to the conclusion that we shouldn't take our own emotions or even ourselves as a whole into account, which is precisely why social media is a double-edged sword.

In a sense, social media is a highlight of people's lives - Not the entire story.

Listening To Your Own Feelings

So how do we battle this? Social media is far from the only perpetrator of lowering self-esteem, but it is also a great example of one because most of us use it daily.

Regardless of if you're talking about a bully you had in your class or some stranger's opinion on the internet, you probably can't do much to change the negativity that is being thrown your way, and you shouldn't have to.

Negativity will always be a part of our lives the same way positivity will always fight it back.

Instead of changing the outside factors (a task which can not only be exhausting but is sometimes plain impossible), what you can do is focus on what's under your control - your own perception.

By listening and understanding your emotions, you become the master of how those negative people or things affect you.

An excellent first step is to ask yourself questions - as much as you can and as often as possible.

Get to know yourself more, understand why you like what you like, how different things make you feel when you are happy, what makes you sad, what you want to hear when you're in a bad place, your hopes, and dreams, etc.

For instance, the questions you can ask someone you want to be friends with are almost identical to the ones you can ask yourself and you should focus on your answers just as much as you would if it were a different person giving them.

What this process of asking and answering your questions does, is it switches your focus from the outside world to your inner reality.

With this shift, you start understanding why your feelings and thoughts have just as much value as everyone else's and why your opinion is just as important.

After that, it's much easier for you to share the emotions and ideas you have with the world.

You see, when you truly understand something - its origins, its current form, and its future effects, you are more confident when you are facing it as well as when you have to explain it to someone else.

The same way you find explaining simple things to kids easier than untangling complicated theories when you have all the answers using straightforward language, it's much more comprehensible both for you and for your audience.

In addition, this newfound conviction that comes with knowledge allows you to be more open and truthful and therefore attract the proper response.

From that point on, everything is pretty much smooth sailing.

Take-Home Message
This first step to learning to take your own feelings into account is hard and takes some getting used to.

Nevertheless, it is vital in bettering our opinion of ourselves and the importance we give it.

By learning to take your emotions into account, you will undoubtedly find out new things about yourself, how to pay attention to them, and why you couldn't see them before.

This form of self-realization and the change that comes with it is something that everyone should experience because it brings you closer to the person you ultimately want to be - a person who truly understands themselves and is happier for it.

LIMITING BELIEFS & HOW TO DESTROY THEM

The human species is the most complex being known to man, due to the extended neural network we all have.

This highly evolved nervous system allows for complex thought processes, deep emotions and the ability to manipulate matter more than any other species we know of.

And though it appears that we are all demi-gods on planet Earth, we all have our own limitations, which stop us from achieving our best life or even being the best version of ourselves.

In this chapter, I'll give you our insight on limiting beliefs and how to work through them, so without further ado, let's get to it!

The Human OS

Just like smart devices (computers, smartphones, etc.), we humans also have an "**operating system" (OS)** we run on.

For smart devices, that may be Windows, iOS, Android or whatever else, but in our species, that operating system is called "**mindset**".

Your mindset is made up of belief systems, which determine your interpretation of the world around you.

Besides that, the mindset you're in will cause a loop which I like to refer to as the "**Think>Feel>Behave**" loop.

Example: You are low on money and your rent and bills are due soon	
Thought	"I don't have much money, I'm screwed, there's nothing I can do."
Feeling	Desperation, scarcity - You're about to hit rock bottom
Behavior	You ask someone to lend you money / You start selling items of yours / You open up a line of credit

Now, certainly, asking someone for money or opening up a credit line can certainly save your butt, but really, think about it - Is that the only option that exists in the world?

Probably not.

What Are Limiting Beliefs?

Limiting beliefs are basically any thoughts and opinions which appear to be the absolute, objective truth in your experience/situation.

These are essentially the things that keep you away from achieving your goals, whether they are financial goals, fitness goals, etc.

Now, in the context of greater achievement, limiting beliefs are something bad, but at their very core, limiting beliefs are your brain's best bet.

Your brain, in fact, ALWAYS expects the worst, so that it can deal with whatever comes its way.

So to a certain extent, limiting beliefs are a survival mechanism that has evolved over millions of years.

However, nowadays we live during the safest time possible and even more so, the time with the greatest opportunities available globally.

That is to say that in the 21st century, limiting beliefs don't really protect us, but rather block us from achieving our true potential.

"The only thing that's keeping you from getting what you want is the story you keep telling yourself."
Tony Robbins

The Origin

Now, though limiting beliefs may have a negative impact on your personal and professional success, we are not really trying to guilt trip you here.

Even the most successful people have those limiting beliefs and it is a life-long quest to get over them.

The first step, before you try and destroy them, is to understand the origin of your self-limiting beliefs.

In the book "The biology of belief", Dr. Bruce Lipton explains how most of our self-limiting beliefs are developed throughout our earlier years (up to 7 years old).

During that time, the brain works in wavelengths that are very similar to those in a hypnotic state.

In other words, as kids, we are open to information, take everything for granted and accept it as the truth itself.

During our childhood we develop beliefs of all kinds - Ones that support our growth and character and also, ones that limit us from achieving during later stages of life.

The Quest

Those limiting beliefs we all hold only manifest during the later stages of life, when we have to take care of ourselves and work for our own development.

After your teenage years, your quest is to recognize and work through those limiting beliefs, in order to update your human OS and achieve any vision you may have.

In the second part of this article series, we'll give you our actionable tips to help you bash through the door of limiting beliefs and create the best version of yourself possible.

There's more in the next chapter.

Notes:

LIMITING BELIEFS | PT. 2 - SHATTER YOUR BARRIERS

In part one of this article series, we learned that limiting beliefs are thoughts and opinions which we believe in, which is the main reason why they keep us away from achieving more.

Those limiting beliefs are mainly developed through our earlier years, where our brains absorb information like a sponge, in order to create a logical mental model of the world.

Now, though limiting beliefs are functional to a certain extent, they are not the best bet in the context of becoming the best version of yourself.

In this chapter, I'll give you actionable tips and tricks which you can apply on a day to day basis, to shatter your limiting beliefs and progress further.

How To Shatter Limiting Beliefs

If you catch yourself unable to take action on certain ideas, thoughts and visions, it is more than likely a matter of mindset.

And though limiting beliefs may persist throughout your experience, they are not necessarily something permanent, as long as you have the desire to work on them.

The mindset is flexible and it can take on a multitude of belief system configurations so needless to say, your experience is nothing but the end product of the story you keep telling yourself and believing in.

Here are our best tips to shatter limiting beliefs

#1 Embrace Challenge & Change

The fixed/limited mindset will always look for shortcuts and won't recognize the value of real effort and challenge.

Another common trait of the limited mindset is the desire to always be in a flow of sensual pleasure, thereby making effort & work look even less attractive.

However, if you accept that effort isn't fruitless and that you can change for the better, you will instantly become more prone to taking on more challenging tasks.

Without a doubt, as you persist more and more through challenges, you will see them for what they really are and the idea of fruitless effort will pass.

Effort is the path to personal development.

#2 Toughen Up

In general, people who are bound to their limited beliefs, give up pretty easily for the most part.

Again, this is a product of the perception of effort, which, in a fixed mind, seems like something fruitless.

Well, the truth is that for the most part, giving up is automatic, because you're following the same old behavior pattern.

In the face of setbacks however, you can CHOOSE to persist, instead of giving up.

This will be something unknown for your brain if you've been limited up until that point, meaning that there may be a certain level of resistance.

Nevertheless, if you choose to persist, you will train your brain and create new, more productive behavior patterns.

#3 Observe Yourself

When you acknowledge that most of your emotions and behaviors are automatic, you will come to find that you don't really make conscious choices whatsoever.

Your brain knows what it's going to do and has taken the decision way before the thought of doing it surfaces in your conscious mind.

When you observe your emotions, feelings and behaviors, you have the opportunity to actually make a conscious decision, against that which your brain has taken.

Whether we're talking about relationship behavior, social behavior or just the way you treat yourself, observing all of that and taking different choices at the time of occurrence is the best way to rewire your brain

And Remember…
You will never be perfectly unlimited, simply because we humans always go through more and different experiences, as long as we are alive.

Those different experiences awaken and trigger a multitude of emotions and behaviors, some of which have been buried inside of your brain for decades.

Shattering limiting beliefs is about recognizing the thoughts, opinions and behaviors that keep you away from your best self.

Stay self-aware, make different choices, keep your head up in the face of setbacks and remember that personal development is a life-long quest!

NOTES:

MEDITATING YOUR WAY TO CALMNESS:

Where to Start

Being more mindful, calm, and relaxed will involve slowing down and spending some quiet time with yourself and this is best done in the form of a classical meditation!

Meditating can be a foreign and somewhat difficult practice, especially for those who are constantly rushed, overthinking, and under pressure, but it's a great tool to use to become more serene.

In this article, we'll go over the basics of meditation and how you can use it for your own greater good and achieve an undisruptable state of calmness.

Without further ado, let's get to it, shall we?

What is Meditation?
In short, meditation refers to a practice that involves a neutral state of mind that does not latch onto any thoughts or emotions, but rather observes them.

It is a technique that is used to enhance self-awareness, mental well-being, calmness, and serenity by reducing overthinking, anxiety, and stress.

Though it may seem complex at first, meditation, at its very essence, is really simple, so let's have a look at the actionable steps you can take towards achieving a meditative state of mind!

Where do I Start?

To a certain extent, people may have made meditation seem like an esoteric, borderline magical practice.

This leads to the belief that meditation is something hard to do and certainly, it may seem like it is not for everyone.

Luckily, however, anyone can do meditation as it interacts with the brain and its different modes of work and thought patterns.

To make it easier for you, we've broken it down into a step-by-step process, so let us have a look!

Step 1: Setting

Before you start meditating it's important to find a quiet spot where you are able to sit and relax without being disturbed - a closed room, a quiet spot in the garden, or a communal meditation class will be perfect.

Many experienced in meditation like to burn some incense or candles and play relaxing music in the background - ensure that the room temperature isn't too hot or too cold and that you have a comfortable cushion or chair to sit on.

All of this will allow you to focus less on sensory information and more on your inner world.

Step 2: Timing

Beginners should start meditating for a shorter period of time - set the timer for 5-10 minutes and increase the daily time limitations as you get more accustomed to the practice.

Some people meditate between 30-60 minutes on a daily basis, but this doesn't mean that you have to do it all at once, you can divide the time between morning and afternoon.

Ultimately, the goal is to lose track of time - Don't over-fixate on the time spent meditating, but rather the quality of the meditative state.

Step 3: Become Body Aware

Once you've comfortably nestled into your meditation spot, it's time to notice your body - Close your eyes and become fully aware of your physical body while closing your eyes.

During this pre-meditative state, you should make sure that you are feeling comfortable.

You can also bring your awareness to all body parts, starting from the toes and working your way up.

Step 4: Breathing & Heart Focus
Once you've made sure you are comfortable and in a calm environment, it is time to get to the core of your meditation - Breathwork & heart-focus.

Breathing is one of the key ingredients to a successful meditation session and though it is not mandatory, it is a powerful tool that can easily induce a meditative state.

Breathe in deeply through your nose, for 3-5 seconds, pause briefly and exhale slowly, taking the same time that you took on the inhale.

Focus on this breathing pattern - 3-5 seconds on the inhale and 3-5 seconds on the exhale.

In the beginning, you will consciously breathe like this, but in just a couple of minutes, this breathing tempo will become automatic.

While breathing slowly, focus on your heart and notice how it works - If you come to a meditation from a stressful work day, your heartbeat may be quicker.

Try and release every bit of tension with each exhale and bring about a powerful relaxation signal.

In doing so, you will be able to calm your heart down - Notice how the heart rate drops, the more you continue with your slow breathing pattern.

Throughout your meditation session you should be focusing on your breath and the sensation of air filling your lungs and then leaving the body, as well as your heartbeat.

In a full-on state of meditation, your breath will be slow and deep and your heart will do less, but more powerful beats.

Step 5: Keep Track of a Wandering Mind

Contrary to popular belief, the goal of meditation is not to turn off your entire thought process.

At one point or another, your mind will start wandering, which is why, the goal of a meditation is to just pay attention to this when it happens and CHOOSE not to follow any thoughts and make them into a story.

When you are focusing on your heart and lungs and an intrusive thought comes to mind, try to swipe it away and bring your awareness and focus back to your lungs & heart.

Step 6: End on a Kind Note
Once your time for meditation has run out, end the session in a gentle manner by taking a moment to notice your surroundings - the sounds and the sights.

Be kind to yourself in this moment and notice your own thoughts, feelings, and emotions - even if you are still feeling a bit stressed, you can continue practicing meditation every day until you reach a calmer general state of being.

Even though meditation can be quite tricky in the beginning, it becomes quite simple once you practice it more often - you just have to start somewhere!

Bringing yourself into a calming state is important for a healthy body and mind, meditation is your first step to serenity.

Find a quiet spot, take a seat, close your eyes, and start breathing and remember, with time, meditation will become a STATE which you can maintain throughout the majority of your wake life.

MOOD SWINGS | PART 1 - DEFINITION & CAUSES

Understanding The Dynamic Nature Of Your Emotions

Thanks to experiments and proven theories, we now know that the entire universe is constantly searching for balance, trying its best to avoid extremities at all costs.

Similar to the pendulum of a clock, we, like the universe, constantly search for the golden middle.

We do this both consciously and subconsciously in pretty much every aspect of our lives - work and rest, spending time with friends and alone, working out and relaxing.

We do most of the basic human activities with the idea of establishing a balance between them.

This is why, when your emotions are stronger than normal, it can feel challenging to go about your day as you usually would.

Although mood swings are common, we aren't always sure why they happen and how to control them exactly.

Sometimes the intensity of our current emotions doesn't have an explanation, and we find ourselves questioning everything that surrounds us.

This is not only exhausting but can sometimes have a more lasting negative effect on us, our relationships, and the overall quality of our lives.

For those and many more reasons, I've decided to shed some light on how to understand your feelings better and take the first baby steps towards establishing control over them.

What Do Psychologists Say?
Certainly, whenever we have an acute change in the state of an individual, there will be a bunch of psychologists trying to explain it.

So here comes the question-

What Are Mood Swings, Exactly?
Psychologists identify mood swings as great and sudden changes in the current emotional state of an individual.

When you quickly go from feeling happy and upbeat to being easily irritated and blue, you are likely experiencing precisely this phenomenon known as a "mood swing."

Sometimes mood swings are a part of an underlying condition, and sometimes they are the side effects of the many challenges we deal with that are a normal part of life.

Why Do They Happen?

The most common reason for mood swings is... You guessed it - Stress!

Regardless of whether it's sudden and extreme or accumulated over time and seemingly negligible, stress is the most common cause for rapid changes in our emotions.

When we are under pressure, we can't focus on keeping everything in check, and we sometimes neglect our feelings, resulting in them spiraling out of control.

This is precisely why we sometimes end up experiencing random shifts in how we feel towards certain people, events, and topics.

Significant life changes are also widely known to cause shifts in mood.

Whether this process happens subconsciously or not, we often respond more emotionally to things when something big is currently happening in our lives.

For example, getting married, finding a new job, becoming a parent, moving to a different city - all these things have a resounding effect on our temper and perception.

This phenomenon makes sense in the world when you think about all the emotional thoughts we have while experiencing such events and all the pressure and excitement they often bring us.

Mood Swings As A Symptom

One of the lesser-known things is that mood swings are also a part of almost all mental illnesses - depression, bipolar, and borderline personality disorders are just to name a few in which rapid changes of mood are extremely common.

This information should be considered by the patient and the doctor treating these conditions because it may change the final way of dealing with the problem.

Mood swings can also accompany Alzheimer's, strokes, and other conditions that affect the brain.

Hormone changes are also a common cause of mood swings.

For women, the hormone estrogen often has this effect which is dispensed during the menstrual cycle and pregnancy, and for men, that can usually be caused by testosterone and other major hormones that also undergo a cycle.

Regardless of whether you are undergoing hormone treatment or just the body's natural response to something, a hormonal imbalance in your body can often make you feel emotions more intensely.

Medication As A Cause

A different reason for experiencing these fluctuations is if you are using certain medications or are in the process of changing your prescription.

For example, mental health medicine often has this side effect, especially if you take it for the first time or change your usual routine.

This is because it is designed to work with the part of your brain which deals with emotions, and there is a period of adaptation in which the brain gets used to the change.

However, other types of medications can be a reason for mood swings, and you should ask your physician if you are experiencing this and believe it's because of your prescription.

How Common Are Mood Swings?
Most people experience mood swings at least a few times a year.

This is completely natural because they are often subconscious responses to things that happen to us, some of which are beyond our control.

We are incredibly emotional beings, and as such it's impossible to expect this part of us will always be under our absolute control.

As a matter of fact, trying to keep everything under strict management is often why we end up having mood swings in the first place.

With that being said, if you are experiencing them a lot more often and they hinder your life in any way, you should ask for the advice of a professional as it may be a symptom of an underlying condition.

Nevertheless, before doing that, take a look at the next chapter where I go in-depth on the steps you can take towards successful emotional management.

MOOD SWINGS | PART 2 - MANAGING YOUR EMOTIONS

Gaining Control Over The Automatic

In part one you learned more about mood swings, their nature, and main causes.

With that information in mind, you are now one step closer to resolving any emotional issues you may hold deep within.

Why you may ask?

Well, because to resolve a certain problem completely, you don't need 'just a solution'.

You need an understanding of the core of this problem and why it arose in the first place.

As a matter of fact, this deep understanding can also lead to logical conclusions that highlight the exact path towards the resolution of the problem at hand.

Nevertheless, having concrete cues as to the methods you can use to manage mood swings and your emotional states, as a whole, can also massively help!

In this second part of the article series, we'll cover just that.

And so, are you ready? Let's start!

Maintaining A Steady Mind

If you've read some previous materials on our blog, you have probably seen us mention that the modern-day lifestyle and social dynamics can easily kick your mind off-balance.

In a world like this, it is crucial to establish the skills necessary to keep your mind steady, in order for you to be able to guide it to whatever path you are looking to take.

Based on experience, we would say that this has 3 main aspects:
- Stress management
- Lifestyle choices
- Different perspectives

Let's start with the most important one - Stress management!

Stress Management
Alright, if the most common culprit for mood swings is stress, then it makes sense for the easiest fix to be stress management.

Depending on the kind of stress you are experiencing, you may need different types of solutions.

For instance, if you are under extreme momentary discomfort, you can try different breathing techniques.

However, yoga may be a better idea if you are dealing with stress that has accumulated through time.

Whether you find it peaceful to be alone or with people, managing stress is absolutely possible and will ease the shifts in your mood.

And yes, yoga and other exercises can help, but stress management is done on a level of perception at the deepest level.

So, whenever you experience a stressful situation, try to stay aware of your reaction to it and start questioning it.

Because reactions involve a great level of emotional output and are automatic, we usually follow their sequence.

But suppose you use your most powerful tool. In that case, awareness and consciousness.

And you use that to question the automatic behaviors, well then, your emotional reactions will change over time, thus leading to less prominent mood swings.

This is base 1. From then on, you have to get back to your natural human patterns, and your emotional transformation will be complete!

Let's have a look at the lifestyle choices you can abide by to resolve mood swings!

Lifestyle Choices

As I mentioned, your lifestyle choices massively impact the internal chemistry your body is running on.

Bad chemistry means poor emotions and poor emotions mean more frequent mood swings.

Think of it this way - Your body was designed to work in a certain way (that we call 'natural') and if you get further from that (which the modern lifestyle pushes us towards), well, you know what happens.

So let's have a look.

You've Got To Move It Move It
Ah, yes, exercise.

When you are consistently active, the machine your body is starts working in the best way it can because it has the best incentive it needs.

Not only that but exercise also releases endorphins that are responsible for regulating stress and overall mood.

By teaching your body to be consistent, your mind will likely follow and naturally start fighting rapid shifts in mood.

Even just a 30-minute workout once every two days will positively affect your emotional state.

Oh, and not to mention, you will start looking better naked as a side effect.

Think of it this way - The body was DESIGNED to move! Just look at your complex musculature - It's begging for you to get up and move so that the body can fulfill its true potential.

So get up. Sprint. Climb. Jump, crawl and swim - Find a way to move that you love, and stick to it!

Consider Tai Chi and/or QiGong

Wake Up, Sleepy Eyes!
Getting the amount of sleep you need with the quality you need is synonymous with feeling like the normal you.

We have all had sleepless nights or experienced difficulties when trying to do something taxing early in the morning, and we all know how that made us feel.

Sleeping well is vital for the way you perceive the world and therefore what emotion it incites in you.

This is why people that have chronic problems with sleep often have mood swings.

So try this:
- Go to bed at the same time
- Avoid eating heavy meals right before bed
- Avoid screentime in the last 1-2 hours before bed (try listening to soft meditation music)
- Create a bed routine

Eat Like Your Ancestors

If you're not getting all the nourishment you need, you may experience negative changes in your mood.

This is why some people are cranky in the morning - lower blood sugar and caffeine withdrawal (if they drink coffee daily) can make a person easily irritable.

Malnourishment works in the same way but on a deeper level - food is the body's fuel, and you can't expect it to work properly if it doesn't receive what it needs.

This is also why some digestive disorders are associated with mood swings (pssst, it's all in the gut!)

Certainly, though, eating well nowadays is something very hard to do, mainly because we are constantly bombarded with ultra-processed foods.

Nevertheless, that doesn't mean you can't find food close to the natural quality that our hunter-gatherer ancestors had.

Here are 7 of our best-rated foods everyone should focus on:
- Grass-Fed beef
- Eggs From Pasture-Raised Chicken
- Wild-Caught Salmon & Other Seafood
- Dairy Products From Pasture-Raised Animals
- Root crops (carrots, potatoes, beetroot, etc.)
- Fruits & vegetables
- Nuts

Besides focusing on those, one should also avoid highly processed foods and if consumed, they must not represent more than 10-15% of an individual's total daily food intake.

Just Ask Someone!

If you are worried that your mood swings are a sign of something deeper or just have trouble dealing with them easily, you should seek the advice of a therapist.

There, you will find the answers to all your questions and start working on a plan to keep your emotions in check.

Different types of therapy offer different solutions, and you will undoubtedly find one that suits your needs.

Two of my top recommendations, though, is Cognitive Behavioral Therapy (CBT), because this strongly relates to one's perception about things, and this is precisely where the change is made and the other is Neuro-Linquistic Programming (NLP)

Final Thoughts

Mood swings are a common problem for many people, especially in today's fast-paced society.

This is exactly why you can find a lot of information about them and advice on dealing with the challenges they pose.

Although sometimes such seemingly random shifts in your emotions may seem scary or make you feel powerless, it's crucial to remember that there is nothing you won't learn to handle with time.

Start with small changes to your daily life and see where they take you and how they make you feel, and always know that you can get help the moment you feel you want to.

Stay balanced!

Notes:

MORNING ROUTINES FOR A SUCCESSFUL DAY

Everyone desires a successful day as being successful is one of the humans' highest wishes, now that we live in a world beyond just survival.

While it may seem hard to achieve, it is highly possible, all you need to do is condition your body and mind to do certain things.

Your mornings can determine the dynamics of your whole day, which is why it is a good idea to practice the right morning routines.

In this chapter, I will discuss the morning routines you can use to kickstart your day and make it YOURS!

What does it mean to have a successful day?

Yesterday, today, and tomorrow are all the same except for what is done on each of these days.

Yesterday may have been rough, tough, or unpleasant, and today may not be looking good, however, tomorrow can be better depending on what you do TODAY.

A successful day isn't necessarily the one during which you made a lot of money or achieved something amazing.. It is often one which you can look back on and smile because you feel fulfilled and satisfied.

Having a successful day means that all plans made for the day were accomplished and you are fit to progress by looking forward to the next day.

A successful day starts with an accomplished morning ritual, as the beginning of the day sets the tone for the remaining part of the day, as we mentioned already.

If your mornings are usually boring, inactive, degrading, the rest of the day will probably carry this vibe on.

If your days haven't really been fulfilling recently, you need to look into the things you do in life and more importantly, in the mornings.

On this note, here are four-morning routines for a successful day.

Four Morning Habits For A Successful Day

So what does a morning routine for a successful day really consist of? Well, a set of mental and specific habits, which you too can develop!

Let's see.

1. Early rise from bed

Wake up with determination. Go to bed with satisfaction." Rising early from bed is one of the practices that will enhance a successful day.

Since "An early bird gets the worm," it means that if you want to achieve all your plans for the day, you need to wake up early and get to them - This will help you get everything done quicker, with more ease and earlier, leaving you a window of time for yourself.

Some people get their days messed up because they don't get up early enough.

Getting up early provides you with enough time to prepare for the day, and creates stability for your mind.

Furthermore, sunlight governs many processes in the body and the spectrum of light during the earlier hours of the day, close to the sunrise, are highly beneficial for us.

2. See to personal hygiene and immediate chores
A healthy body leads to a healthy and refreshed mind which will lead to high productivity; hence, seeing to personal hygiene is vital.
When you are clean from head to toe, your hygiene is taken care of, and your clothes are neat, there's a sense of calmness that clouds your mind.
Being clean prevents you from becoming a nuisance to those around you.
On the other hand, immediate chores such as tidying up where you slept, washing up dirty plates, or putting dirty clothes in the laundry may help with keeping a healthy and organized mind.
As above, so below, as within, so without.

3. Warm-up for the day's activities

To achieve proper wakefulness and prepare yourself for the days' activity, there is a need to warm up for the day.

Warming up includes exercising, meditating, eating breakfast, greeting those around you, watching the morning news, engaging in some light inspirational reading, playing some brain-tasking games, or other activities that keep your mind active.

Remember that as soon as sunrise hits the horizon, you're bound to get out of the state of drowsiness and into the fully awake and alert state that allows you to seamlessly go through your day.

4. Go through your to-do list
Before sleeping every day, it is advisable to keep a to-do list for the next day.
Keeping one helps to plan your day and keep you focused to achieve a successful day.
In the morning, go through your to-do list to remind yourself of the things you need to achieve for the day and set new goals if need be!

Conclusion
There are certain habits you can adopt in your morning routine, but in the context of having a fully successful day, you must remember one thing…
That is namely the fact that success and happiness are an internal state.
So maintain that state and stay open for more physical and mental growth, progress and well-being!

This page purposely left blank for your notes

MOVING OUT OF YOUR PARENT'S HOME - IT'S TIME

You know how sometimes in life there is a moment when you realize that things are going so great. Like the train is on the wrong track, the decisions you make, or don't make, don't seem to make you happy.

Well, If you're in your late twenties and still living with your parents, that's the reason.

I'm not saying It's wrong to do so, I'm saying that It's not healthy for you to be still drinking beer outta their fridge and creating a human sized cavity in their sofa.

If you have some of the things listed below then you've outstayed your welcome and should start packing ASAP.

Still unemployed and working on it?

Life is always shifty - one day you have a great job and you feel on top of the world , the other you're counting your pennies and feel as small as the ant that's been living in your kitchen.

Things happen and it's not your fault. Except for the scenario where you live with your parents and casually can't find a suitable job in the last couple of years.

We all procrastinate. It happens, but not facing the fact that It's time to grow up is a serious issue. It's hard and It's scary and It needs to be done.

You should do it for yourself, It would just feel so rewarding when you make your own money and have a place all for yourself.

Struggling with self confidence?

The home is a safe space, a sacred place where you are the one calling the shots, judge, jury and executioner. You don't know what I'm talking about? The reason may be, because you still rely on your mother to cut the crust on the sandwiches.

Still living with your parents can surely create a gap in your confidence towards your actions, words, decisions and thoughts. It's a living hell for making life choices.

A good idea would be to make the biggest decision for now - find a new place!

It's not your fault?

Excuses are a pretty typical human reaction when It comes to doing something you don't want to do, or don't have the attitude to do. That's no reason to blame someone else for your laziness.

I admit, parents can be overprotective sometimes. They would smother and baby you just so you don't fly the nest. Even if that's the case, you shouldn't let excuses guide your life.

It may seem that the coziness of the bed you grew up in is irreplaceable, but believe me It is a huge trap. Let yourself experience life by jumping out of that comfort zone and into the unknown.

No one is responsible for your life's actions except you, don't forget that.

Living on your own is scary at first. You sit in the quiet room, knowing that you are nowhere near your home, It is possible that you would cry a little bit. It's normal.

There is no reason to be afraid of taking the first step towards your independence. You need it, you are not living your life properly without being independent.

The tough times teach us to appreciate the good ones and make us stronger. You can't get that from the couch.

If you fall even slightly in one of the categories you have to do something about it. Do it for yourself. Do it, because It's scary. Do it to prove to yourself that you are more than a twenty something year old that is still asking his father for gas money.

Life is not scary, you not living it is!

Life is not scary, you not living it is!

SELF CONTROL

To suffice, I term self-control or self-possession as self-discipline. It's a term used to describe a person's ability to control themselves, the power to restrain rash responses and behavior, as well as to keep unhealthy attitudes and impulses in place.

As other people may say, this quality of character is not a negative or restrictive trait. Self-control becomes one of the most powerful methods for self-improvement and task achievement when it is available and used carefully and in common sense.

Self-control is essential for managing obsessions, fears, addictions, and impulsive behavior of some sort. It allows you to take command of your life, your actions, and your reactions. It strengthens your bonds with others, cultivates patience and tolerance, and is an important tool for achieving prosperity and happiness.

BENEFITS
So what makes self-possession such a powerful trait if developed to its maximum potential?
You develop a strong sense of self-discipline and willpower to tackle the hard tasks and life obstacles.
You can easily address your fears and weaknesses
You develop patience with life and people
You'll never be lazy; thus you achieve more
You improve your social life as well as your personal life

HOW TO HARNESS SELF CONTROL

ALTER YOUR BELIEFS

Recognize the emotions and values that cause you to act out of control. What attitudes and emotions trigger automatic instincts and reactions? Is it someone around you?

Reduce impulsivity and rash responses by identifying these feelings and opinions, attempting to clarify them, and determining if they are rational and attractive.

VISUALIZE

Visualize yourself exercising self-control and discipline in your actions. Imagine yourself behaving professionally, with self-mastery and restraint in one of the situations where you normally act out of control.

Keep this picture in mind, but ensure you don't obsess.

PRACTICE

By this, I mean being self-disciplined. If you focus on improving and growing your willpower and self-discipline by appropriate workouts, it will increase significantly over time as small efforts build to become significant leaps. This is the most crucial step in the development of this delicate attribute.

PRACTICE AFFIRMATIONS

Repeat one of the affirmations below for a minute or two several times a day, particularly when you need to demonstrate self-control: I am fully in command of myself, I can control my feelings and thinking, Self-control gives me inner power and propels me forward, My emotions are under my influence, My actions are under my control, I'm learning to regulate my feelings, I am the mastermind behind my life's maser, My capacity to regulate my emotions and thoughts is improving day by day, and Self-control is pleasurable and enjoyable.

IDENTIFY

With this last step, figure out where in your life you need to improve your self-control. Or else, where do you find yourself missing the mark?

What areas of your life do you find yourself deficient in this ability? Is it overeating and junk food consumption? Shopping addiction, excessive abuse of drugs, gambling, binge-watching, and so on.

This way, you can set accurate goals on the tasks you're aiming to achieve, and this way you can achieve more accurate results.

BOTTOM LINE

I'll throw it straight to you; nothing worthwhile is going to come easily and so is your ability to control yourself. It takes time, so be patient and consistent. (I confess, I am still working on this myself)

SELF-MERCY VS LAZINESS – WHAT'S THE DIFFERENCE?

Many times, we get so occupied with work and responsibilities that we forget to take care of ourselves.

When this happens, we attempt to find the time to cool off and pamper ourselves, which is where the concept of "self-mercy" comes in.

However, some people believe this to just be used to justify laziness...

For example, taking the weekend off work to binge your favorite Netflix movies as a form of self-love.

While this may be the case, oftentimes it is an excuse to procrastinate and be lazy.

Though the line between self-mercy and laziness is thin, they are different concepts.

Self-mercy is a necessity and should not be confused with laziness, so let us dive further into this.

What is Self-Mercy?
Self-mercy is taking care of oneself and showing yourself appreciation and compassion. It is the process of holding yourself in high regard and prioritizing your happiness and well-being.
This is not about gratification as in laziness, rather it motivates you to maintain practices that are beneficial for your physical and mental well-being.
It is the perfect way to ease stress and stay productive.

How to Practice Self-Mercy
There is no standard rule for this, it all boils down to preferences and that which brings out your best.
Do those things that spark your creativity, improve your mood and enhance your growth.
Here are some simple steps for you.

Outline what you intend to achieve, as this will influence your ability to properly integrate self-mercy.
Divide these goals into long-term and short-term and brainstorm activities that can move you towards them.

To become accustomed to self-mercy and make it effective, turn it into a habit.
Incorporate it into your daily and weekly routine, and soon enough it becomes a part of you.
Pace yourself and start small so you don't get overwhelmed.

Tune out all forms of distractions and listen to your body, it will inform you when it's time for resting and pampering.
(This is the purest form of self-mercy)

You probably shy away from self-love because you believe it is exhausting. Understand that you deserve every form of kindness and find ways to make the process easier for yourself.
You could find an accountability partner to help with this.

What is Laziness?
As stated earlier, it is easy to confuse laziness with self-mercy. Whereas self-mercy is a means to recharge for increased productivity, laziness is the act of avoiding tasks that you should be doing. It reduces motivation and hinders us from reaching our goals.
If you still can't differentiate the two, here are the signs of laziness.

When you procrastinate, you constantly put off priorities and focus on less important and non-beneficial tasks.
This is a challenge faced by many people, and they waste time on unproductive things that prevent them from accomplishing their goals.
A lack of self-discipline is one of the major causes of procrastination.

Practice will make you know the difference between taking needed time off to recharge, and avoiding important tasks because you were not in the mood.
The latter is laziness and will leave you with a sense of guilt because you wasted the time meant for more important activities, the time you will never get back.
To avoid this, plan your self-mercy activities.

Doing nothing at all is a sign of laziness, you do not exercise, read, or do any other activity that can contribute to your growth.
Instead, you stay indoors all day ignoring your assignments and things that do add value.
It is easy to cross the line from just the appropriate amount of self-mercy time to getting fatigued from taking too much time off due to laziness.

Conclusion
Self-mercy is the innate ability to recognize the right moments to take a rest and recharge your batteries.
Nevertheless, that does not mean completely relaxing and not doing anything productive, but rather, opening up time for active recovery.
Self-mercy can be a challenge at first and may lead you to become lazy without you even realizing it, but once you've established a clear border between the two, your self-mercy will allow you to perform better mentally and physically.

Notes:

SIGNS YOU'RE EMOTIONALLY WELL

Of course, nicely-shaped muscles are attractive, but there is a far greater sign of good health than just a fit body: emotional well-being.

Your emotional health has an impact on every aspect of your life, and caring for it is just as essential as caring for your overall physique.

How can you tell whether you're in great emotional shape? Continue reading for indications that you value your health on the inside and out.

You are grateful in all parts of your life daily

Gratitude is the source of all happiness, and cultivating a grateful heart is a proven way to attaining emotional stability and well-being.

The willingness to appreciate any positive thing in our lives is a significant indicator of emotional wellness.

Reaching a state of thankfulness might seem like an exercise in futility if we have a negative attitude or low mental stability.

If you're having these types of issues, take baby steps. Find something to feel thankful for in your life. Make a list, and then at least two things you need to be thankful for the next day.

You are considerate of others
Compassionately seeing others and engaging them with selflessness and goodwill is a sign of personal well-being.
This is referred to as prosocial behavior by psychologists. It indicates you're sympathetic to other people's feelings and needs, and you believe it's vital to aid them.
It entails helping people in distress, even for things as easy as returning a misplaced purse to a receptionist or grinning and engaging the next person on the queue in a friendly conversation.

You take pride in who you are and the person you are becoming.

When you are stable emotionally, you are pleased with yourself. You are acquainted with your flaws and talents, and you're comfortable with who you are on the inside.
Also, you are consistent, which implies that the personality you present to the public reflects your core self.
Consistency in this context means that the overarching feeling of your essence is in alignment with what you project to the outside world.
Although there are instances where you instinctually shift your behavior or attitude due to social circumstances.
Consistency suggests that your overwhelming view of your innate self is in harmony with what you project to other people out there.

You repair and forgive relationships that have been damaged
Getting bitter isn't constructive or healthy, and a mentally healthy individual understands when it's time to let go of ego and power if they must rebuild a strained connection.
Although not every relationship can be repaired, attempting to at least hear other people's side of the story is considerate and sensible.

You place a higher value on memories than on belongings
You see yourself valuing vacations, events, and dinners with friends over material goods, choosing the ethereal to the physical.
The same is true for social networking sites. An individual in good mental health will devote considerable time appreciating an event rather than attempting to capture it for others to see.

Your Life Has A Purpose!

Having a purpose, a goal, or a broader significance for your life is what it means to live a meaningful life.

This occurs when you apply your skills to aid a cause you care about. Working with children, becoming engaged in politics, becoming an active member of a faith community for a worthwhile purpose are just a few examples.

Conclusion

Emotional wellness is more of a process and a continual effort than a destination.

When we achieve a sense of balance and psychological well-being, we must nurture and build it as much as we do with muscles.

Of course, It requires time, effort, and a firm commitment to be resilient and emotionally well.

You're far more powerful than you think, you're competent, and you're deserving of feeling mentally healthy and empowered, no matter when you're on this path.

TESTING THE WORTH
OF YOUR WORDS

Why Putting Yourself In Trying Situations Is Beneficial
People that are extremely honest are always a source of inspiration.

Being able to trust each word they say and knowing you can count on them are abilities most of us look up to and strive for.

The reason why we feel so deeply for people's honesty especially if it's backed up by their actions is because that way we can build a trusting relationship with them.

If one can always be truthful, blunt, and honest, one's presence, opinion and actions are always felt and appreciated.

In order to be this type of person, however, you must be sure of where you stand, and this happens by testing your beliefs and ideologies and proving them right.

This is why testing yourself is so important.

The Different Personal Qualities Taking Risks Improves

By putting yourself in unfamiliar situations, you inevitably learn things both about yourself and the world.

This expands your field of vision, and because it's a hands-on experience, it is much more likely for you to remember all the things you were taught in the process.

Learning from experience has proven to be the easiest way most people acquire new knowledge, and by testing your beliefs and thoughts, you are provoking such types of situations.

Not only do you discover new aspects of the world and yourself, but it is also highly likely for these actions to avalanche, leading to newer and more interesting people, places, and experiences.
- Bravery

Figuring out where you stand on different topics is crucial to building your worldview.

This can be hard if you limit yourself to doing pretty much the same thing every day.

By getting out of your comfort zone, you openly fight this way of thinking and improve your chances of having the courage to do so again.

Bravery is taught by challenging yourself and facing your fears, and the best aspect of life this can be done in, is precisely, personal development.

Learning how to push yourself to your limits in order to progress and by doing so, moving those limits away even further is how you enlarge not only your comfort zone but your world in general.

This is not to say that you should be reckless in any way, simply that progressing further in life implies moving forward in it and taking risks, every now and then.
- Honesty

The people closest to us are usually the ones with whom we are always honest and who do the same for us.

The people we believe in and the ones we look up to the most are also the ones that are the most honest.

This is a quality that simply does not have a negative side in the grand scheme of things, but it can be hard to keep this mindset under challenging circumstances and situations.

By learning to do so, we learn to trust ourselves more, and we teach others that they should do the same.

The senses of freedom and self-worth one has when they know they're being completely truthful regardless of the outcome, play a big part in building our character the way we would like to.

Different Ways You Can Improve These Qualities
•   Think Critical & Leave Room For Improvement

Thinking critically of your own thoughts might sound negative, but in essence, it is the exact opposite.

By figuring out every aspect of your views and ideas, you gain a full personal picture of yourself and can see why it looks the way it does and where things can be improved.

It is much easier for you to change your mind if you're uncertain of why you think the way you do, and similar situations are often regretted later.

If you think critically you not only avoid the negative possibility mentioned above but know exactly where you can improve and can ask for advice for that specific aspect.

Both realizing why you think this way and what you would like to change are equally important. Both take time and honest analysis of yourself but once you've done that everything is much more organized and easier to understand.
•   Ask yourself if you are standing up for what you know you think

This step comes after you have passed the first one.

The easiest way to keep yourself in check regarding what you believe is to simply ask yourself this question.

All of us have been in situations, which we have later regretted because we weren't completely honest and this is the only way to avoid them.

It might be hard to really hear your own voice in the beginning but it's always worth it in the long run.

Once you understand your thoughts and beliefs, standing up and defending them in their entirety is the next logical step.

It's advantageous to question your words and actions, not because you doubt them but because that way, you recognize how much you believe in them and are willing to fight for them.
•   Put yourself in trying situations to expand your horizons.

Once you have everything else down, expanding your world is the best thing you can do.

By pushing your limits, you find new horizons, ideas, emotions, and more.

Not only does this solidify your ideologies, but it makes room for more character-building and bigger adventures.

By breaking out of your comfort zone you allow yourself to see the world for what it is and can start doing what you love and be honest about it.

Thinking of life as something to explore and learning everything you can in the process is crucial to becoming the person you want to be, and the only way to achieve this is to expand your worldview through actions.

Overall, testing yourself is never easy.

Questioning your points of view and realizing some of them aren't as solid as you thought they were, can be a difficult experience, but it ultimately is the best way you can progress. Wisdom is NOT knowing everything, wisdom IS knowing and admitting when you are wrong and having the willingness to learn what is true.

Understanding your thinking and why it is that way makes it easier to act the way you want to and build yourself into who you want to be.

Keeping yourself in check about being honest is helpful because we are not perfect, and sometimes we make mistakes, but if we catch them early, it's easier to work on and fix them.

Exploring the world by getting out of your comfort zone is what makes us progress and achieve what we strive for, thus providing us with the full experience of what life is and what it has to offer.

Although all of these things are not a walk in the park, I believe they are essential in making us the people we want to be, and by doing them and making them a part of our mindset, we are one step closer to what we want to achieve in life.

This page purposely left blank for your notes

THE STAGES OF PERSONAL DEVELOPMENT

Personal development is a vast topic, which has many stages and involves a lot of continuous effort through time.

There isn't really a thing that will set you for life through a short burst (well, maybe there is but just financially).

In the context of character growth, personal development is a life-long quest with no end point.

We learn, as long as we are alive and curious enough to absorb more and grow.

In this chapter, I'm going to talk about the stages of personal development and how to recognize and work with them.

Don't Look For Shortcuts

The vast majority of people want to have it easy in life, without realizing that proper personal development is a system that has many stages, which require a certain amount of time and effort.

Shortcuts for short-term goals are the usual mindset for many people becoming more aware of their personal development, while in reality, it is nothing but a long-term process.

Now, the main concept of personal development and growth is to acquire new knowledge, new skills and to go out of your comfort zone.

Think about it, no one achieved something great by being warm and cozy, right?

The Stages Of Personal Development

As we already mentioned, personal development is a process that goes through different stages, all the time.

Stage #1 - Self-awareness

For the most part, people act in a predictable way, repeating the same actions, feelings, thoughts and emotions.

Once you become aware of those though, you have the opportunity to start analyzing yourself.

That exact self-analysis is the fundament of personal development, as it helps you learn more about yourself, your needs and interests.

Think of this as your inner compass.

Stage #2 - Comparison

Once your personal development starts giving you results, you may find yourself being more social and observing/analyzing other people.

From that analysis comes the comparison between you and your peers, making it easy for you to differentiate between the different types of behavior, which produce certain results and outcomes.

More often than not, such social behaviors and interactions, may lead to a good value exchange - You learn something from someone and vice versa.

Stage #3 - The point of no return

When you eat the fruits of your labor, you are in stage 3 of your personal development process.

During this stage, you break through the mental barrier and start thinking about all the things you can do to make your life better, along with the life of others around you.

During this stage, you start learning new knowledge and skills exponentially fast and get a burst of inspiration.

Stage #4 - Acceptance

Once the curtain of your limiting beliefs and thought patterns is pulled away, you are in a limitless mindset.

In your head, you can achieve anything and everything, but you now know and accept that even though sudden bursts of inspiration do happen, the process requires discipline and dedication.

This is where you have to further look through your priority list, modify it, set short and long-term goals and plan everything out, pen on paper.

End Quote

If I had to summarize the essence of this chapter in one single quote from a person who's been through stuff, it would be this one:

"When you focus on being the best person you can be, you draw the best possible life, love, and opportunities to you."

— Germany Kent

THE AREAS OF PERSONAL DEVELOPMENT

"What lies behind us and what lies before us are tiny matters compared to what lies within us", says Ralph Waldo Emerson.

Almost every successful personality has given utmost importance to personal development and growth.

They have depicted personal development as a pathway leading to skills, attributes, and qualities needed to live an efficacious and prosperous life.

Personal development is defined as a lifelong process. The Business Dictionary defines it as, "The process of improving oneself through such activities as enhancing employment skills, increasing consciousness and building wealth."

Personal development involves self-care which includes all those activities that help us to evolve in our self-best.

As George Bernard Shaw once said, "Life isn't about finding yourself. Life is about creating yourself."

Personal development is not something that can be achieved overnight; rather , it's an evolving process that includes several steps.

Starting from establishing our personal vision of life to understanding where we are now. Once we are able to comprehend our current standing then we can move ahead, and identify the areas where we need to work.

The Areas of Personal Development
There are several areas where we can start grooming ourselves for personal development. These areas are: physical, social, mental, emotional and spiritual.
Let's go over them one by one.

Physical Development
A healthy body and a healthy mind, two essentials to ensure before taking on an expedition/ journey, whether it's an actual, physically-demanding journey, or your life journey!
Our physical well-being is an important ingredient in leading a blissful life. It's not only about doing exercise, rather it's about having a balanced diet that includes proper nutrition, getting proper 7-8 hours of sleep, and maintaining body weight and BMI levels.
When we are physically fit, we tend to have more energy and we can utilize this zealous energy in achieving our life goals, seamlessly.

Social Development

Smiles are contagious, so are positive vibes. Living in a society that demands social interaction and effectively communicating with people can help boost our self-confidence and self-esteem.

Talking to different people not only helps in enhancing our confidence but also awareness of worldly scenarios.

People we connect with play a vital role in our lives as they implicitly impact our thought processes and moods.

Therefore, interacting with the right people, learning new languages, and active listening can be helpful in our own development and growth.

Mental Development

When we learn something new, our brain tends to generate new neural pathways to hold onto the information.

Mental development is most important in personal development because it helps to create a cushion for new skill sets and qualities to develop.

Mental development activities include reading a book, taking online courses or training, or watching informational and motivational YouTube videos. Not only these but also relaxation, keeping our mind tension-free can help in boosting our mental activity.

Emotional Development
Many people nowadays are more focused on Emotional Quotient (EQ) rather than Intelligence Quotient (IQ).
This is perhaps, because people with high IQ might not be able to survive under high-pressure situations whereas people with high EQ are seen to be more stable, focused, and better achievers.
In today's fast-paced environment, it's necessary to be emotionally stable and not be hyped by unanticipated circumstances.
Emotional development can be done via having a counselor/therapist, journaling things down, or even, talking to a friend!

Spiritual Development

People often confuse spirituality with being religious, whereas one's religion has nothing to do with being spiritual.

Spiritual development involves being fully connected to all five senses of our body. It is about synchronizing our doings with our thought processes. It is about creating coherence between our body and soul.

Spiritual development can be achieved through yoga, meditation, or praying if you are religious. A deep connection to your soul is a deep connection to your awareness, which enables you to recognize and take on the correct actions towards achieving your ultimate personal development.

Take-Home Message

You are not just a body, nor a brain… And quite frankly, you are not just a soul.

In fact, you are an intricate mix of all those things, and this is perhaps why you, as a human, are able to do and feel so many things.

Personal development is a life-long journey that simply represents the goal of improving your mental, physical, spiritual, emotional and social development, thus enabling you to achieve the best version of yourself.
And so, are you ready for your new, best self?

HABITS TO IMPLEMENT IN YOUR LIFE

As humans, we are creatures who think, do and say out of deeply embedded habits.

Each habit can either be productive or destructive for our long-term personal development, health and well-being.

In reality, if you think about it, your current life situation and state of being, are a direct reflection of the habits and thought patterns that you sustained and acted upon.

Without a doubt, habits play a big role in our lives, as they are a vital part of our behavioral patterns, which in turn lead our lives in certain directions.

A Bad Habit

Breaking up with your bad habits and implementing new, more productive ones is without a doubt one of the toughest things to do.

This is something that requires strong willpower and the desire to actually break the habit of being yourself.

As we already mentioned, these habits, even the more toxic ones, feel natural, because they are what the brain knows.

The quest is to break those patterns and establish new, more productive habits.

At first, this may feel unnatural but rest assured, the more you do the unknown, the more it becomes the new known.

Here are some ideas for new habits you can establish to improve your overall quality of life

#1 Exercise

Besides making you look good naked, exercise can help you perform better in every aspect of your life.

Every time you do weighted or aerobic exercise, a flurry of nourishing substances is unleashed, which in turn improves the function of both your muscles and the brain.

These substances include dopamine, serotonin, endorphins and oxytocin, all of which create euphoric states that make you feel more content with everything.

#2 Eat Whole

Your well-being is a result of the way you treat your brain and your body.

The things you put in your body (food, liquids) play a big role in all functions of your organism.

It is important to remember that there are essential nutrients for the body, that we need but can't produce on our own, internally.

The most essential nutrients are protein and fats, which are best derived from quality, well-grown animal meat and organs.

While animal products should be at the core of your nutrition, you can include servings of vegetables and a carbohydrate source (potatoes, rice, other grains, etc.) to every meal.

Besides that, a couple portions of fruits a day, will also provide viable micronutrients, which will improve the functioning of your body.

Focus on whole foods!

#3 Be Grateful

Though very important, exercise and nutrition are not all there is to health.

The mental state you're in will, to a big extent, determine your perception of each experience.

A healthier perception of life means better overall well-being which therefore implies that mental practices can be introduced to your lifestyle, especially if you have a tendency to be more negative.

We spend a lot of our time digging through problems and while for the most part they look negative, problems help us thrive and improve.

Try and shift your focus and perspective to one that makes you grateful for everything, even your problems.

Gratefulness allows you to feel content with what you have, instead of feeling the lack of what you don't have.

This natural mental state of abundance will, in turn, put you in a position where you can utilize it to take action on what needs to be done, in order for you to have what you want/need.

#4 Be in Solitude

People are social creatures and as such, many of us tend to always be surrounded by people.

However, just like some philosophical teachings suggest, the biggest breakthroughs come in solitude.

This is why it is important for you to have meetings with yourself, to analyze experiences, create a mental map of the future and last but not least, unwind from the overwhelmingly social world we live in.

Remember, life is not all about goals and achievements.

Sometimes you have to take a seat back, relax and look at things from a third perspective.

#5 Read

As cheesy as it is, reading is one of the best habits you can implement in your lifestyle.

Think about it, people write books when they are at the peak of their creativity, when they want to share something with someone.

Books are the best way to gain knowledge from people that have been through things, and also the best way to train the creative/imagining part of your brain (i.e fiction books).

Conclusion

At your very core, you are a very complex, biological deep-learning machine, which you write the code for through your thoughts, emotions and behaviors.

For the most part, your daily life is 95% automatic, which is the exact reason why you should consciously engage in creating new and better habits.

Recognize and target your bad habits and try to replace them with things that support the work of your body and brain!

This page purposely left blank for your notes

THE IMPORTANCE OF SELF-LOVE:

Tips on Being Kinder to Yourself

If you are reading this, I have no doubt that you are a kind and compassionate person, but just as much as you are kind to others, you have to be kind to yourself as well.

Practicing kindness towards yourself gives you the power of self-acceptance, self-compassion, self-love, and general personal growth.

All of these are important throughout your life's journey, so if you are interested in learning how to love yourself more, keep reading.

Why is Self-Love Important?

There are many reasons why self-love is important, all of which relate to your relationship with yourself, as well as others.

Here are just a couple of the reasons why self-love is important:
- Teaches you to embrace yourself just the way you are
- Gives you the ability to forgive yourself for any mistakes in your past
- Lets you move on from past trauma
- Increases self-worth
- Making it easier to let go of what you might think is 'imperfections'
- Improves sleeping habits by dealing with anxiety and depression struggles

Tips on Being Kinder to Yourself

Without a doubt, being kind to yourself is easier said than done, especially if you have already developed self-sabotaging habits like negative self-affirmations or self-punishments.

Nevertheless, it can all be reversed for your own greater good, so let's have a look at the actionable tips you can take on!

Give Time to Yourself

At this moment you are probably dedicating more time to your job, family, and friends than you are giving to yourself... And this is something normal but quite frankly, it is not sustainable so you should change it!

Take time throughout your day to do something that you love doing, whether it is painting, walking through the park, baking, playing an instrument, or just taking a long warm bath, it's important to have some 'me-time'.

Time spent out of productivity and into enjoyment is your opportunity to reflect on everything else and make the necessary adjustments.

Take Credit

Give yourself recognition for your accomplishments, when you achieve a small or big goal you have to celebrate yourself, bring the bubbly and praise yourself!

Instead of waiting for recognition from others, you should give yourself a pat on the back when you do something that you can be proud of.

You deserve it!

Fuel Your Inner Advocate

We are all our own worst enemies and are sometimes harder on ourselves than anyone else is - your inner critic can be super judgmental and it has to be silenced.

Try to go one day without criticizing yourself; instead of fueling your inner critic, rather cultivate the little voice in your head that stands up to criticism and defends you - your inner advocate.

This requires a different level of self-awareness, as the inner critic is usually hardwired and has already established a believable (negative) story about you.

Get over that!

Embrace Your Good Qualities

What are your good qualities? Write them all down and embrace them as your strengths while cultivating them to be even stronger.

Even though you might not have the best temperament in the world, you make up for it by having a keen eye for detail; focus on your good qualities and they'll overshadow weaknesses.

Daily Affirmations

In the same way as our bodies are a reflection of what we eat, our minds are a reflection of the thoughts and information we put in there, too!

Give yourself daily affirmations like, "I'm Enough!", "I'm Worthy!", "I Deserve the Best!", "I Can Do It!".

Making these positive phrases part of your daily life, will have a drastic effect on how you see yourself.

This works because an affirmation, repeated enough times, can literally rewire your subconscious habits on an emotional, physical and mental level.

Accept Yourself

Every single person has faults and victories, weaknesses and strengths, good characteristics and bad habits - embrace yourself for all that you are: the good and the bad!

When we stop criticizing ourselves for our faults, we can be much more accepting and content in our own skin - accepting yourself is the greatest form of self-love and should be reinforced every day.

The Self-Love Movement Continues

Self-love should never be misunderstood for selfishness or self-obsession, a lot of self-love is a very healthy part in the relationship you have with yourself.

The great thing about continuing this movement and implementing methods to increase the love for yourself, is that it will spill over into others' lives.

Don't be shy, give yourself a big hug and some much-needed love and share that with others.

Make self-love contagious.

Notes:

THE TWO MINDSETS - COMPETITION VS COOPERATION

Which Mindset Can Get You Further In The Game Of Life?

Mindset, mindset... And mindset again! Oh, the wonders it does.

Would you describe yours as a competitive or cooperative mindset?

Well, in case you are anything like me, the answer varies.

For example, when I was younger, I was always very competitive in martial arts, not so much these days after sustaining back injuries, but my "competitiveness" is still there.

But when it comes to friendships and other types of relationships (hint: especially business ones), I believe that it's crucial for us all to cooperate so we can be of mutual benefit.

The two mindsets may seem different, and as if you are bound to just one, but truth be told, they both serve a purpose, and the key is knowing which one is needed at certain points in our lives!

Sometimes we need to be more competitive because it brings out our best qualities and pushes us to succeed, whereas other times, we need cooperation because of relationships we have with others who will help us get where we want.

In this chapter, I'll discuss both mindsets and their main characteristics, and in the second part, I'll tap into the more practical question - Which one should you abide by?

And so, are you ready? Let's read!

Survival Of The Fittest

In 1859, Charles Darwin published "On the Origin of Species"

He was one of the first people to continue developing this theory that had been previously proposed and, in this case, been furthered by Mr. Darwin himself.

The ways in which Charles Darwin's views on evolution have contributed to how it is currently theorized, by the way, I don't believe in his theory of evolution, I believe in a God who created everything, but Mr. Darwin did make one valid point...

The point is that nature is all about competition - It's either I eat you, or you eat me.

According to the theory of evolution, survival is based on how fit you are for the environment you live in.

If you're not fit enough, you'll get consumed by the fitter, stronger species in your environment.

And well, looking at nature, that does make sense in some ways.

Perhaps, this theory is what instilled in people the belief that life nowadays, too, is a game of "survival of the fittest" - This is what gave rise to the so-called competitive mindset.

What Exactly Is The Competitive Mindset?

The competition mindset is all about winning.

It doesn't matter if you win by stealing, cheating, or just being better than the other person.

The point is that you win, and that's it!

There are no second-place winners in this game of survival of the fittest.

This type of thinking has been around for a long time because it makes sense for people to want to be on top and stay there.

After all, we're living in a society where success equals power.

But while striving to be number one may work sometimes, it can also lead people down a dark road which will only end up hurting them in the end.

Hint: If you eat everyone on your way to the top, you'd have no one to celebrate with?

So what should we do, is the question here?

Well, let's take a look at cooperation...

The Cooperative Mindset

The cooperative mindset is about working together to accomplish a common goal.

This type of thinking has been around for many centuries, and it's not just limited to humans - Animals also engage in cooperation.

In fact, different types of cooperation can very well be observed, even in nature where it's considered that everything is competition-based!

But what does this have to do with success, one may ask?

Well, it's pretty simple - Having a cooperative mindset means that you're willing to work with other people and put aside your personal goals for a while for the sake of achieving a collective one.

In other words, if you're looking for success, then don't forget that it can't live outside of healthy relationships!

After all, there's no real meaning behind the word "success" if it's being used without a single reference to helping other people reach their goals as well.

Yes, many people consider themselves a "one-man army," but in reality, you are never really alone.

If you feel like you've achieved something entirely by yourself, odds are you fail to realize and give credit to the side contributors to your success. (even if they're passive)

Jump over to part 2, where I touch on interesting details about this topic, such as the traits of the two mindsets and how to integrate them!

See you in part 2!

Notes:

THE TWO MINDSETS:

Competition VS Co-Operation

Part 2

Traits Of Competitive People & Why You Should Rely On Compassion

People are always thinking about competition. Whether it's at their workplace or in their personal lives, people always want to be the winner.

This competitive mindset is present not just in the world of sports but beyond it, as well. Though effective in some regards, this mindset has its drawbacks that can lead to suboptimal results both personally and professionally.

Instead of constantly seeking ways to beat others, we should learn how to cooperate with our peers for a greater chance of success than if we were trying alone.

Nevertheless, in some instances, the competitive mindset has its applications and may, in some cases, bring out the best in you!

And so, are you ready to learn more about the mind? Then, let's jump straight into it!

Traits Of A Winner

As we just mentioned, many people (especially in corporate environments) are highly competitive individuals looking to be the shark in the small tank of fish.

From the moment they wake up to the moment they sleep, they're constantly thinking about how to beat everyone else that is around them.

Following this train of thought, we can conclude that the main traits of people that have adopted the competitive mindset are:

- Egocentrism

As we just mentioned, competitive people are focused mainly on the win, and nothing else matters for them, really!

This implies that such individuals are highly egocentric, meaning that they focus primarily on the self.

- Determination

Perhaps one of the most positive things about being highly competitive is the sheer determination to achieve set goals.

Competitive people are not deterred by obstacles and will often go above and beyond to make sure they come out on top.

As mentioned, this determination can be seen as a positive trait, as it can help them achieve great things in a personal aspect.

- High levels of energy

High levels of determination imply high energy levels because, well, a winner has to do whatever it takes to come out on top!

This restlessness and borderline hyperactivity are perhaps among the most obvious traits that can tell you a person is more inclined towards the competitive mindset rather than the cooperative one.

Being Competitive - The Side Effects

Okay, as we learned, some people have a naturally competitive nature.

They thrive in the face of competition and love to see their opponents fall.

But they may not realize that this mindset is actually a detriment to success because it can lead them to do less than ethical things to win.

Even more so, this type of person also has trouble understanding why others reject what they want at all times and will often be very dismissive or even aggressive if someone does not agree with them.

In short, competitiveness can create enemies out of friends and discourage friendships from forming in the first place.

It also makes you more likely to become an egotistical bully who tries too hard for validation and does not know when enough is actually enough.

Integrating The Competitive Side

As I mentioned already, the competitive mindset isn't to be excluded completely.

Instead, one must learn how and when to utilize the competitive mindset and when to properly use the cooperative one.

What this means is that the competitive mindset too can be useful in certain instances.

When competing in a race, for example, a competitive mindset can be beneficial.

It can help you focus on your goal and push yourself to achieve it, with high levels of energy and determination.

This is just one example of a situation where the competitive mindset can be helpful.

However, outside of actual competitions where a winner is announced and you have opponents, well, the competitive mindset isn't really useful.

Because most of our life depends on inevitable communication with other human beings, it is best to go beyond the ego, wants, and needs and focus on compassion & cooperation.

Compassion & Cooperation

Unlike the competitive one, the cooperative mindset is beneficial in many different regards.

When we approach life with a cooperative mindset, we are able to see the world through a more compassionate lens.

We are also better able to connect with others, forming meaningful and lasting relationships.

Additionally, the cooperative mindset allows us to be more effective and productive employees, team members, and leaders.

We are better able to work together towards common goals, and we are more likely to achieve them.

Following that train of thought, we can conclude that the main traits of cooperative people are:

- Compassion

- Generosity
- Borderline selflessness
- Tolerant
- Helpful
- Empathy

And in most cases, that is better than egoism, intolerance, callousness, unhelpfulness, and vengefulness.

Final Thoughts

All in all, it is not always about winning and achieving your desired, ego-related goals (i.e. coming out on top above everyone else).

The cooperative mindset leads to a more harmonious and peaceful world, while the competitive one is more likely to create boundaries between humans.

For this exact reason, we should remember that life isn't a death-match, free-for-all game, really.

Think of life as a co-op game, seek out YOUR best team and see what you, together, can do towards a common goal!

Be compassionate. Be cooperative. Spread love

Notes:

UNLEARN THESE HABITS

Unlearning is the new learning in the journey of having a blissful quality of life. People say, learning a new good habit can be cumbersome but have you ever tried to unlearn a bad habit?
It is much harder to unlearn a bad habit. We, as humans, catch up on bad habits very quickly and let them settle just as our second nature.
There are some habits that one should totally unlearn to grow and stimulate better life decisions.

Fear Of Change

You don't have to be happy about everything that happens in your life. However, you should not let your fear stop you either.

We are all aware that things could be much worse at any time in our lives. Also the fact that you are reading this article right now proves that you are some of the world's wealthier and more privileged individuals.

Life is changing way quicker than ever before, and we may be confronted with new problems every day.

As a result, the most capable of adapting individuals will always win in the long run.

It's much harder than it sounds, but it's probably one of the most underappreciated words of advice.

Even if changes are uncertain, they almost always have a positive aspect.

Be brave, focus on the positive aspects, and try new things.

Procrastination

No matter what your age is, you will always end up procrastinating! We procrastinate because we subconsciously believe that the task ahead of us is too difficult.

So, next time you're in this scenario, make a habit of breaking down your activity into smaller, more manageable chunks.

Delaying something inevitable in your schedule is never beneficial, it only ends up making the timetable more congested and leaves you with greater stress than what you already had. Therefore, always aim to complete your tasks on time and stop procrastinating to let go of the habit of procrastination.

Comparison
Comparing yourself to others is not only disrespectful of your own capabilities but also a total disregard of others' status.
Being jealous of others' achievements without knowing what they have been through in their actual life is never justified nor advised.
Never compare yourself with others. Always compete with yourself and beat YOUR previous best.

Being Afraid to Make Mistakes
Isn't making mistakes just an aspect of our human nature? Everyone makes mistakes but there are very few people who accept them and rectify them.
Following the notion of hard work will always lead to success is one of the biggest mistakes that people make.
Try to embrace your mistakes and it's okay to make them. Never go too hard on yourself for making mistakes and instead, try to learn from them.

Obsessions with Other Peoples' Opinions

How often do you feel discouraged because of the opinions of others? The chances are that your answer is too often.

The scary part is that you will never be able to appease everyone. The good news is that it makes no difference.

You only have one life, so don't bother wasting it by trying to live up to the expectations of others. You can't be everyone's favorite, but you can be your own hero and save yourself.

Stop suppressing your inner voice to please others and start shining your light on the world.

Start unlearning bad habits and learning the ways to improve the quality of life.

No matter what your definition of quality of life is, just make sure to enjoy every moment and reap the utmost benefits from every day that you are living.

Notes:

WANT TO UNLOCK
YOUR PURPOSE?

Here's 3 Ways You Can Do So!

Everybody needs a purpose in life, something that motivates them to get up in the mornings and embrace the day; a reason to live, love, and laugh!

Finding your purpose is extremely important because it will influence and guide your life's decision, your goals, your behavior, and your sense of direction.

In this chapter, I'll give you 3 actionable tips on how to identify and get on your own purpose.

But before I do that, let's answer a very important question…

What Is Life's Purpose?
If we look at life objectively, we can conclude that every living organism is technically a community of trillions of cells.

All those cells have one simple purpose - To survive and eventually reproduce.

In the modern-day human world however, we live way beyond survival and thus, start looking for more meaningful goals that reflect and bring about a greater purpose.

Usually this greater purpose is linked to certain dreams, goals and aspirations in our minds.

Having a sense of purpose has been scientifically proven to improve mental and physical health, since it is adaptive and evolutionary throughout the course of your life.

For this reason, NOT having a purpose can be quite destructive to anyone's life, so let's have a look at some of the things you can do to find and unlock YOUR purpose.

3 Ways to Unlock Your Purpose
Your purpose is not something you pick, really. Instead, it is something that kind of "unlocks" during the process of introspection & analysis of one's life experience.

Here are 3 ways you can unlock your purpose quicker!

Some studies suggest that those who give will experience a great sense of meaning in their lives, whereas happiness is moreso linked to taking.

When you give your time to a charity organization by volunteering, share your talent with others, or donate money to helpful causes, you will feel a great sense of meaning and purpose in your life.

Doing something kind for someone in your community is the first step to unlocking your purpose in life; whether it's handing out meals to the homeless, showcasing your art, or giving some of your riches to those in need.

Keep on giving your time, talent, or money to different causes and your path will follow a natural road towards your purpose.

Many people go through life without knowing themselves, having no idea whatsoever about their interests, weaknesses, strengths, or even how their behavior affects their circumstances.

In order for you to unlock your potential, you have to be more self-aware and the only way you can do that is by exploring your own personality and interests.

Explore your personality by becoming more self-aware during anything that you do and furthermore, ask your friends and family for feedback.

Ask them for their honesty on how they perceive you and your behavior, so you can get an adequate 3rd person perspective!

Most of all, discover what activities you enjoy most and whether you actually like the occupation you are currently in; these things are usually a reflection of your passions, skills, and talents.

Think of it this way - Throughout your life, you've collected the pieces of a puzzle, but you've lost the box and can't possibly see the end result without putting the pieces together.

If you are stuck in a rut and it feels like your life has no meaning, then you have to get out of your comfort zone and try new activities and pastimes.

Are you regularly engaging in conversations on certain topics or activities without having actively participated in these things before? You might just want to actually try it out!

When you enjoy talking about history or gardening with friends, why aren't you taking history classes or pursuing a little green garden of your own?

Stepping out of your comfort zone might be a bit strange at first, but you'll be one step closer to unlocking your purpose if you get out there and try new things.

There are TOO MANY things that you'd love doing, that you don't even know of... Go experiment and find them!

Unlock Your Purpose Now!

Unlocking your purpose isn't something that can be done in a few short days or hours, it's rather a lifelong journey of discovering and exploring your interests, behaviors, personality, and way of life.

Pause what you are doing and just reflect on your daily routine- Is it leading you in a direction that serves your purpose or that gives your life meaning?

It's never too late to unlock your purpose in life, no matter how old you are, so go ahead and dive within to find it!

Notes:

WHAT IS THE GROWTH MINDSET?

If we put things black & white, we'd realize that the majority of humans come to this world with the same "specs", so to speak.

We all have a brain, body and all our bodily systems work on the same principles and run the same chemistry.

But what is it that actually makes a person successful and different from other people?

Well, the secret, perhaps, lies not in lucky circumstances, but in the mindset, which in turn controls our actions and reactions.

Think About It…

If you look into your own life, you may come to realize that though you are creative, your mindset has probably, at one point, had a big influence on you and your overall success.

Contrary to popular belief, skills and knowledge are not a given, but are rather developed through time.

How Important Is Mindset, Really?

Now, setting bad luck and unsuccessful ventures aside, I can tell you one thing - Your thought patterns lead to certain actions and behaviors.

Even more so, your thoughts and feelings are literally the CODE of your brain's workings.

Whatever you think about, you attract and find more of!

For example, if a friend or a colleague starts talking to you about a potential business idea, do not instantly start talking about why it can't happen.

If you fix your mindset on the reasons why it cannot happen, you will only find more and more reasons why it can't happen.

Instead, try and think of those things as "obstacles along the way to success", rather than "reasons why it cannot happen".

Now obviously I'm not telling you to be delusional and emit fake positivity about projects, relationships, business ideas, etc.

What I'm telling you is that you should consistently put in the work to shift and transform your own mindset to "What is the solution for this?" rather than "Here's why this is impossible".

Fixed Mindset VS Growth Mindset
Before transitioning and transforming your mindset to what I call "growth mindset" you have to become aware of your current mindset about certain things.

In most cases, we, people, have limiting beliefs about many aspects of our lives.

These limiting beliefs cause us to stagnate on one level of development, which in turn leads to the inability to outdo yourself.

This is EXACTLY what the "fixed mindset" is!

Here are some traits of the fixed mindset:
- You give up easily
- Putting extra effort in feels bad
- You don't see how you can further develop your skills
- You stay true to a certain set of behaviors
- You don't take on new ideas/ventures
- You don't take risk
- You can't take criticism

On the other hand, you have the "growth mindset", which implies that you are always a student in the school of life and your skills/knowledge are always due for change and improvement.

The growth mindset, at its very essence, is the belief/feeling that we, ourselves, are in control of our personal development, skills, knowledge, opportunities, etc.

Here are the most common traits of the growth mindset:
- You are always in for extra effort and it feels meaningful
- You always take on learning new skills/knowledge
- You analyze your behaviors/emotions and work on them
- You take risks
- You listen carefully and don't react emotionally when someone is giving you criticism
- You seek to network with people of higher standards/more successful individuals

Take Home Message
Establishing a proper feedback loop, while taking risks and challenges, is essentially at the very core of the growth mindset.

These are the things that attach meaning and actually make you feel like it is worth doing.
Remember, the fixed mindset only sees the problems, while the growth mindset sees the problems and their solutions.
The fixed mindset sees extra effort as unnecessary, while the growth mindset is always in the works.
Stay on your game.

WHEN TO SAY "NO" TO ALCOHOL?

Alcohol has always been one of the major social supplements in the cultural heritage of many nations.

Starting from the ancient Greeks and Romans, the Vikings, the Gaelik tribes, the Germanic tribes, the Thracians, the Conquistadors, the Discoverers of the New World and all the trading with alcohol that goes on even to this day.

Most of the celebrations of major events include an additional glass or two. Going to the pub with your friends, opening a bottle of wine in a restaurant on a date with your beloved, having a glass of aged liquor with your family on occasions.

But eventually there comes a time when you don't realize you've had enough and crave it on a daily basis. This is the time we have to talk about saying "no".

Why Do We Drink?

It is generally considered that alcohol helps us have a good time. The reason for that is the amount of dopamine that the body produces that makes us feel more alive.

The incentive - sensitization theory suggests that not only drinking frequently can produce dopamine, but the association with it does the trick, too. This means just being in a bar, seeing someone open a bottle of wine, etc.

The truth is that overtime the amount of dopamine obtained from drinking fades away, but the amount from the cues stays the same. You drink more to get the same amount of dopamine and ergo - addiction.

Saying "NO" Is The Right Thing

It is true that alcohol reduces negative emotions, but It also reduces positive emotions, as well. Objectively speaking - you numb your brain dead.

Contemplating your life's decisions can get you thinking - Why on earth am I doing this in the first place?

There is always the social side of the coin, which is peer and beer pressure. Both are different names for practically the same thing, which is mostly directed with adolescent drinkers.

The social pressure of being in a queue and not knowing better most of the time leads to starting to drink to be pursued as "one of the gang".

Time goes by and you start to wonder why you are even doing It. It doesn't even bring you joy, just a rush of dopamine to get you through the night.

This is exactly the time to cut down on alcohol, and I mean cut down hard. Nothing good will come of it and your body will thank you for this decision.

The Benefits

After cutting down on the amount of alcohol you consume you will see the results as quick as the dawn breaks.

Mood swings, that you didn't even know you had, will vanish and the feeling of a more productive attitude will rise. This productivity will definitely help you control your craving by giving you the will and energy to exercise more.

Losing weight is another great benefit to getting rid of alcohol from your life. Beer, wine and spirits contain a lot of calories that your body cannot process, which leads to gaining water weight and you can't get rid of that just by running a few laps.

Dehydration, liver problems, bladder problems are other factors that become an issue when drinking alcohol frequently. After cutting down you will feel better and think better.

Of Course, there is no denial that in small amounts some alcohol can be beneficial. Like a glass of wine every night with dinner, or high spirits when having a fever or feeling cold. Just don't let it become a habit.

Fact is that you probably won't become an alcoholic, just remember to listen to your loved ones and never be afraid to seek professional help.

"Wishing" Things Into Existence

PART I - PRIMING THE BRAIN

Acting "As If"

We all know of the law of attraction - positive and negative thoughts bring correspondingly good and bad experiences.

This, in essence, means that whatever you manifest into the world, the same type of thing you'll end up finding in the world around you.

What you probably didn't know is that you can use your brain's powerful abilities to make sure this works in your favor.

In this chapter, I explain how and why this works both on a personal and universal level.

So without further ado, let's get to it already!

First Steps

Alright, alright, before you jump right into becoming a warlock who turns around just to see his 1-second old thought manifested, there are some logical things to do.

Let's have a look at the baby steps everyone should take when considering to develop the skill of wishing things into existence.

#1 Figure Out What You Want

In order to get anywhere, first, you need a destination.

Although this seems self-explanatory, many people aren't all that sure as to what they really want.

This is by no means is a bad state because it allows you to achieve pretty much anything.

However, to actually fulfill any sort of journey, you first have to know where you currently are and where you want to go.

Try asking yourself what some of the core things that make you happy are - they might be places, activities, people, qualities you have.

The list is endless.

Don't limit yourself either with quantity or size here - daring to dream of something is the only possible path to obtaining it.

For example, if NASA had worried about how far the moon actually is, Neil Armstrong would have probably never set off, let alone land.

And just look at where we are now!

Remember that limits primarily exist in your mind and nowhere else.

#2 Identify Ways To Achieve Your Dreams

Once you're sure you've set a goal (or ten;), you can then move on to the next step.

It's essential to look at the big things first. If you're planning a vacation, you tend to first figure out where you'll sleep and how you'll get there and then worry about parking spaces and restaurant reservations.

The same rules apply for any sort of plan - you make sure you have the basics down, and only then do you start sussing out the details.

Personally, I find it really useful to write down my initial core ideas because it helps me visualize them easier and see my strengths and weaknesses.

However, if this doesn't sound like your type of thing, it is in no way necessary.

#3 Believe That You're Capable Of Anything

Some of you might find this part tricky, but it's crucial to progress. The moment you trust you can do something, you can hold yourself accountable and start working towards it.

Think about it - if you need something done, you rely on the people that you believe can actually achieve it, not the ones you doubt could manage.

The same thing applies to you personally - if you trust your own abilities, you know the goal is possible, and therefore you're responsible for its successful fulfillment.

The important word here, "responsible", may sound a bit scary at first, but it's a part of the means which get you to your destination.

As an added bonus, the sense of fulfillment once you've done something you held yourself accountable for is much sweeter than pretty much any other feeling in the same ballpark.

How The Magic Happens

Alright, so you have all these things aligned in your brain, but how and when does the magic happen?

Let's have a look!

The Brain Wants To Prove Itself Right

When you have formulated a statement, your brain's innate desire is to prove it correct.

This means that it will do everything in its power to get you to that specific point.

And, this happens both consciously and subconsciously and is a process on which certain evolutionary improvements have occurred.

Strengthening The Connections Between Certain Neurons

The easiest way to explain this is through neurological connections.

"Neurons that fire together, wire together" is the simplified explanation of this phenomenon.

Picture this as one neuron being responsible for the statement and the other for the action itself.

The stronger their connection, the easier the process - this means that by repeating the statement and supporting it with small activities, which prove it right, more significant positive outcomes will be much more attainable.

Fight Alongside Instead Of Against Yourself

Once your brain is working in the right direction, it is pretty much impossible to experience any form of self-sabotage.

Everything is simpler, faster, and more enjoyable when the connection itself between affirmation and action has become a fact.
This also means that you will grow to recognize and appreciate any progress, which will build up your self-esteem and allow you to aim higher and achieve bigger goals.

It's basically a positive feedback loop, which you, yourself, program inside your brain.

Priming your brain with the right ideas is essential to getting yourself to where you want to be.

Final Thoughts

However it is one of the two main parts responsible for the success of the process.

In the following chapter, I tackle how the rest of the outside world conforms to that to create your personal vision.

The entire universe can work in your favor and how this happens is incredibly curious.

With that in mind, I invite you on an adventure far bigger than us as individuals, but one that is still aimed at improving each of us separately and more to the point, one in which we steer the ship.

And so, are you ready to have a look at the more metaphysical aspect of this?

Read on in part two!

"WISHING" INTO EXISTENCE

Part 2 - The Metaphysical Nature Of The Law Of Attraction
Acting "As If"

In the last chapter, we learned that "wishing" things into existence is not just something magical.

Rather, it is very intricately connected with your brain and its functions - In a way, wishing things into existence relates to your beliefs, thoughts, emotions, and behaviors.

This is where you have to start first.

By changing your beliefs, and I am not talking about your "religious" beliefs, **you influence the sequence of thoughts, emotions, and behaviors that lead to your desired future on a physical level.**

But then again, there are things that happen seemingly outside of you once you internally conform to the desired reality.

These things are what we refer to as… You guessed it - "coincidences"!

The question is, do coincidences exist or are we just using that word to make sense of the unknown reality that happens once we start tapping into the potential of the law of attraction?

Let's Find Out.

The Secret

The Law of Attraction has become a popular topic in the past decade and even has a very popular book behind it, named "The Secret."

Many people have read that and other books about the law and even practiced visualization techniques to attract their desired future into their lives.

But there are many misconceptions about the Law, which might be why some people don't get results when using it.

Let's start with…

The Heart & Brain

One of the most common misconceptions about the law of attraction is that visualization is the key to achieving your desired future.

And while it is undoubtedly a part of the process, visualization is not really the entirety of 'the secret.'

It has been suspected that wishing things into existence is not just a matter of tuning your thoughts, beliefs, and actions into your future, but doing it for **your energy field, as well.**

By "energy field," we don't mean a mystical aura with no actual scientific proof of existence.

We imply the energy field used by certain medical practitioners to measure the function of the brain and the heart.

"Wait, what?! The brain and the heart have a FIELD around them…?"

Yes, that's absolutely right! That field extends about 15 feet in diameter around each of us. And it makes sense because **the body works with electrical signals, and every electrical signal has an electromagnetic field around it.**

The Missing Link
With the above said in mind... Did you know that the heart has a stronger magnetic field than the brain?

And did you also know that the heart has its own brain-like cells that function the same way as the ones in the brain?

This implies that both the brain and the heart hold their very own memories and emotions.

Even more so, it appears that the heart holds the strongest of emotions and may just channel them, to enhance your field ... And attract the like!

The missing link, in this case, is the emotion, which you add up with the visualization to create your dream reality.

Do Your Work & Surrender

When you are trying to wish things into existence, you must accept that your human nature that wants an explanation for everything just may not work in your favor.

Instead, what you have to do is tune in your brain and heart, follow up with them, and surrender to the chance that your desired reality will come in the least expected way, but you will be there at just the right time.

Here's how it works:
- Visualize & FEEL your desired future (Act As If)

This first step allows you to see & experience your desired future ahead of time as if it had already happened.

Since emotions are usually generated after an event has already occurred, a pre-generated emotion ahead of time may trick the brain into believing that the future has already happened.

Therefore, the thoughts, feelings, and emotions you'll have after that fine-tuning will be oriented solely towards achieving your goal.
- Surrender!

Once you take care of your part, which is to tune your brain and heart to feel and act as if your desired future has already occurred, it's time to… Surrender.

Surrender to all the possible ways in which your wish may come into existence.

Don't try to frame, predict and force it into existence.

Do your part and let the universe do the rest because when you do, that unknown, unfamiliar future that you'd otherwise try to predict and create will surprise you in unexpected ways.

Final Thoughts

The law of attraction is a metaphysical concept that suggests you can attract things into your life by focusing on them or as I like to say, acting "As If" in which I mean acting as if what your hoping for is already a reality. It forces your unconscious mind to find a way to "become" that very thing.

This idea has been around for centuries, but it's recently gained popularity in the last few years thanks to its use by celebrities and social media influencers.

However, this belief system is not without skeptics who wonder if it may be just another fad or scam looking to make money off people's hopes and dreams.

One thing is for sure, though - Manifestation is an intimate connection between you, your brain,

AFFIRMATIONS THAT BOOST YOUR SELF-ESTEEM

Affirmations are SO IMPORTANT that I want to discuss them once more just to refresh you.

We've all heard that positivity does wonders when it comes to living the life you always wanted.

Positive affirmations work in a pretty simple way - they build connections in your brain, tricking it to subconsciously prove those assumptions correct.

The science behind it has proof from MRIs, social studies and many different research techniques, proving that although it may sound weird, positive affirmations do work.

These are just some of the wonderful things you can say out loud or in your head to keep pushing yourself forward in the right direction. We recommend you stick to this order, but it's completely up to you and depends on the specific situation you're in.

- Breathe.

This one is very simple, but it does wonders in more intense situations.

It's common knowledge that panic attacks are accompanied by trouble breathing and reminding yourself to take deep, calm breaths is a huge help.

Focusing on breathing itself is a biologically calming process because it slows your heart rate and triggers your parasympathetic nervous system, which is responsible for your body's rest.

- I understand.

This may sound weird to say to yourself, but the more you think about it, the more sense it makes.

In order to push forward in whatever environment and situation you want to, you need to understand the one you're in right now.

A lot of people tend to avoid asking themselves why they do what they do or feel the way they feel and acknowledging both and understanding the reasons behind them is part of progressing further.

When one feels understood, they can get more in touch with themselves and be more honest, thus uplifting the self-worth they have in their own eyes.

- I can do this.

This is essentially pep-talk and when it comes from within it works even better.

Having low self-esteem is synonymous with the belief that you can't do some things and this affirmation battles it head-on.

There are many situations in which a little push is more than enough and hearing these words usually does the trick especially when it comes to situations that have to do with other people, like public speaking for example.

- Take it step by step.

A lot of us feel overwhelmed by how many problems we have on the way to our goals or by how long the way itself seems.

Lacking the self-esteem needed to either take the first step or keep walking the already chosen path is enough to make you quit or to never start in the first place.

This affirmation helps in keeping you focused in the present moment instead of worrying about things that are far far away.

It provides much needed perspective on why your actions right now matter and why you shouldn't give up just because of the road ahead.

- I'm doing great.

What this helps with is retrospective.

Looking back on previous achievements makes you realize how much you've changed, thus how much power you actually have.

It is easy to forget about past struggles when facing new ones, but that doesn't mean that they were less important or less difficult and therefore they hold just as much value.

A different aspect of this affirmation is to appreciate your actions in this specific moment - gaining a third person perspective you can see how amazing what you're doing right now actually is and therefore boost your confidence.

- I can turn my dreams into plans.

This looks only in the far future.

We all have these types of dreams we believe are impossible, but really the only thing that's stopping us is ourselves.

This doesn't mean that the road ahead will be easy, it does however mean that even if it seems nearly impossible, with enough effort it can be achievable.

Changing the word from "dream" to "plan" pushes your brain to think more about how to get you to this point rather than why it seems impossible.

It may sound weird at first, but the world we live in today has enough proof that no wall is unclimbable and that there's no limit to what you can accomplish if you believe in it.

- I love myself.

This will sound weird the first few times you say it but that's no reason to quit.

Such a simple sentence has the potential to turn your life around completely, the moment you start believing it.

It's a journey completely by itself and it may not be easy, however it is absolutely worth the effort.

When you feel love, your entire worldview can drastically change and make a turn for the better, so just picture the power this feeling can have if it comes from within.

This is ultimately the strongest affirmation there is and it really is responsible for miracles.

Although all this may all sound a bit weird at first, with enough consistency it can really help people in building up their self-esteem.

The different perspective these affirmations provide as well as the safe space they build through time are substantial for the environment one needs to cultivate better qualities and self-worth.

You can say them out loud, write them down, read them to yourself or even record your voice and listen to them when you feel comfortable.

There are many more ways you can make this journey fun, for instance write down different reasons why they are true or reward yourself with something small each day you've said them all etc.

I would like for you to try and make positive affirmations a part of your daily life and see how much potential you actually have and how great you already are.

Notes:

DOES PERSONAL DEVELOPMENT JUSTIFY WORKAHOLISM?

Working on our personal development is a great initiative - but have you heard someone telling you that you might be suffering from personal development burnout? Or becoming a workaholic in a not-so-positive way?

Workaholism, by definition, is a compulsive need to work. For some, work is nourished in the womb of life. Upon birth, work brings something important to their life. Like birth, there is necessarily labor, oftentimes painful. Whereas, others are still searching for what work means for them.

If you are searching for what "work" means for you, you must read David Whyte's thought-provoking definition: "Work, after all, is intimacy, where the self meets the world."

Positive workaholism vs. Negative workaholism

The positive workaholism and negative workaholism are often confused. However, if you think you are a workaholic because you love to work on personal development - and if your statement is true then you are more likely a positive workaholic.

Positive workaholism refers to a positive, fulfilling work-related state of mind that is characterized by rigor, dedication, and passion. If you are really into your work then you are a positive workaholic. In other words, not just your skin is in the game; it's your soul that is in the game.

Whereas, negative workaholism has always been about burning out; you put your foot on the gas pedal and do not let up until your engine catches fire. Self-love, contrary to popular belief, is overrated. Things you do during self-love, such as eating comfort food and watching F.R.I.E.N.D.S., are unhelpful; pushing yourself during difficult times may be hard for you, but in the process, a new you will arise and evolve.

Being a positive workaholic entails acknowledging that you cannot rely on your past achievements and must therefore think about the future to see what you can accomplish.

You must keep going

Passion is both the love and the pain of our existence. You can't just pick one without the other. Some people, such as burned-out activists and overcommitted helpers, drown in their sorrowful struggles, forgetting how much they love what they do. Others, such as daydreaming artists and wannabe entrepreneurs, seek out superficial rewards such as fame, fans, and fortune without going through the pain, and thus miss out on the super-rich fulfillment of soulful work.

The large majority of individuals are feeling the walls that stop them from understanding what life is all about, or they are drinking their worries away. But that is not how life works, so you must jump in and flap your hands around until you learn how to swim. You must keep the faith. Workaholics, hustlers, and GaryVee types represent that group of people who aren't concerned with what the other person is doing but are concerned with what they are doing.

Concluding thoughts

Even if personal development provides valuable ways to help you get through challenging times, if you consider yourself becoming anxious, frustrated, and trapped in a cycle of guilt, it's time to recover, reevaluate, and transform what you've been doing so that it works for you. After all, this is your personal development, not anybody else's. It must work for you.

This brings us to the last note, a practical reminder for you: "To begin with, we take only those steps which we can do in a heartfelt fashion, and then slowly increase our stride as we become familiar with the direct connection between our passion and courage." — David Whyte

YES, YOU DEFINITELY NEED A HOBBY

There usually comes a time in a person's life when he or she becomes aware of how little they do for themselves in their free time.

And it's absolutely normal to question yourself because we are programmed to want to know, learn, do more and grow as individuals.

If you've ever felt like you're wasting your free time and all your friends look happier than you, then maybe you need a hobby.

What went wrong?

Don't take it the wrong way, but you probably just got lazy and sloppy.

A lot of people struggle with finding a hobby because of their tight schedules and busy daily routines.

But you can always find half an hour for yourself and your hobby of choice.

Remember when you were a kid, and you used to do all these new and exciting things?

You're an adult now, and you have a job, maybe kids, maybe a dog that needs walking and... less and less energy, perhaps.

This is the right time to start thinking about giving a little bit more than you expect of yourself to start a project, class, sport, or whatever you feel will make you happy.

What can it do for you?

Having a hobby or even a couple of enjoyable side activities can prove to be extremely beneficial for the well-being of both your mind and body.

In other words, it could make you way happier than you are now.

Think of hobbies in terms of "How can I manage my free time in a way that will allow me to spend less time on the couch and more time doing enjoyable activities that will fill me up with energy?"

Engaging in such activities, big or small, will make your day seem more meaningful and put a smile on your face.

It's easier said than done, right? Well, It's not that hard, actually! All you have to do is start somewhere.

To know where to start, however, you need to be aware of the things you like doing or used to do, and more importantly, the things you always wanted to try but never pushed yourself enough to do so.

The idea behind having a hobby is to make yourself feel happier. The way this works is for you to find something you're good at and own it.

Because truth be told, we like doing things that get us recognition, especially from ourselves.

All of this may sound like It's going to cost lots of money, right?

There are actually a couple of hobbies that you can start with to get your blood pumping and ready for the bigger things.

Starting Small

If you don't have a big budget, but still want to make yourself partake in new things you can try starting with smaller hobby choices.

Things like starting a **YouTube Channel** that you upload videos of your passions and interests such as **gardening** or **painting**, or even **cooking** can help you get started with finding your new and exciting hobbies.

The way this helps is that you start to think about time management and finding those extra 30 minutes for something that tickles your fancy.

Not only does this make you go more public, but it also helps with finding out what you may be good at.

Partaking in sports is always a great idea for your body and mind to rewind after, or before, a long day. Yes, it may take a little more time than other hobbies to go to the gym, or for a run, but you won't be sorry for sure.

Reading, writing, and learning new languages are all great and cheap activities that help you grow as a person, grow emotionally, and feel more fulfilled as an individual among peers.

Alternatively, you can always combine some of these activities or do others, but the bottom line should be doing things you like for yourself.

If you don't, then who will?

Take your time to find enjoyable activities outside of work and/or school - Find your own means of enjoying the mind and body you have been blessed with to their full potential.

We have come to the end of our journey for now. I want to thank you for allowing me your time and interest. I hope these pages will serve you well. I do believe that if you take the time and put in some effort that you will see progress in your life. The information within these pages is not just my opinions, they contain the studies and experiences of many researchers, scientists, physicians, psychologists, therapists, coaches, hypnotherapists, and so on.

I am open for discussions if you should have any questions about the content in this book I would also love to hear about any positive changes in your life after reading it. I can be reached by email renewedlifecoaching33@gmail.com

Be Blessed

Dr. Robert John Bonus PhD